1

# P&O180
## the history of
# P&O ⊠ FERRIES

Managing Editor
## Miles Cowsill & Dan Bridgett

Contributors
## John Hendy, Richard Kirkman,
and Bruce Peter

## Ferry
**Publications**

Published by:
Ferry Publications, PO Box 33, Ramsey, Isle of Man  IM99 4LP
Tel: +44 (0) 1624 898445    Fax: +44 (0) 1624 898449
E-mail: ferrypubs@manx.net   Website: www.ferrypubs.co.uk

**Above: The Officers and Crew of P&O's** *Benares* **(1858) photographed in 1862**
*(P&O Heritage)*

# Contents

John Garner and Helen Deeble with the keel coins for the *Spirit of Britain*. *(Brian D. Smith)*

# Foreword

## by Helen Deeble Chief Executive of P&O Ferries

Welcome to this celebration of the 180th anniversary of the Peninsular & Oriental Steam Navigation Company, a brand with a famous heritage and an exciting future.

We at P&O Ferries can trace our history back to 22nd August, 1837, when the company which became P&O signed its first government contract to run a ship delivering mail from Falmouth to the ports of the Iberian peninsula. In so doing, the company helped to foster trading connections between the countries of Europe.

Today, we have more than 4,000 employees who play a vital role in keeping people and goods moving throughout the continent. We carry more than 10 million passengers and two millions units of freight every year, operating more than 20 vessels and sailing on eight major routes between Britain, France, Northern Ireland, the Republic of Ireland, Holland and Belgium.

Although aviation tends to dominate the media headlines, there is a growing appreciation at all levels of government that the services we provide are of vital importance to the transport infrastructure and economies of Europe. This is true not only of the countries to which we sail directly but also of central and eastern Europe, where manufacturers rely on our services across land and sea to export goods to Britain.

Demand for maritime transport is only going to increase and we will ensure that our company continues to be best placed to meet that demand.

The ferry industry has faced many challenges in recent years, from the financial crisis and global recession, to low cost airlines, competition from fixed links and environmental legislation. But the industry has overcome these challenges by listening and adapting to its customers, raising still further its levels of service and improving its value for money proposition.

Everyone at P&O Ferries is determined to extend our unique, 180 year tradition of success for many decades to come.

# Chapter one

# The beginnings of P&O

The *William Fawcett* is generally regarded as the first steamer to run on the company's fledgling Peninsula service. Painted by Stephen D. Skillett in 1836. *(P&O Heritage)*

Like many boys who grow up to be very successful men, Arthur Anderson's beginning was a humble one. He was born at Lerwick in the Shetland Islands in 1792 in a house, today a museum, which also served as a store for the fishing and fish curing activities which took place on the adjacent beach.

Having come into the world within sight of the North Sea, one of the two future founding fathers of the Peninsular & Oriental Steam Navigation Company was always going to look to the oceans for his livelihood. Aged just 11, he was earning his living by curing fish.

His first experience of the open seas, however, offered few hints of the auspicious future which awaited him. The young Shetlander was pressganged into the Royal Navy, serving in the Napoloeonic Wars before he was discharged – penniless – in London ten years later.

But, as so often in rags-to-riches stories, it was here, in the

Above: Arthur Anderson, one of the founding fathers of P&O, painted in oil by Thomas Francis Dicksee in 1850. *(P&O Heritage)*

Right: In 1910 P&O acquired Lund's Blue Anchor Line and operated a Branch service to Australia via the Cape. Poster from 1911. *(P&O Heritage)*

emerging metropolis of the industrial world, that a benign turn of fate was to transform Anderson's fortunes utterly.

A Scarborough shipowner called Christopher Hill, who was later to become his father-in-law, introduced him to Brodie McGhie Willcox, who – although not yet 30 - had recently set up a shipbroking and insurance partnership. The year was 1815, which is now famous throughout recorded history for the Battle of Waterloo.

The embryonic partnership between Anderson and Willcox –

**Above: The *Viceroy of India* (1929) moored at Bizerta, Tunisia.** *(P&O Heritage)*

**Right: Winter tours to India and Ceylon brochure, 1935.** *(P&O Heritage)*

who would in time become the first managing directors of P&O - was to become significant for shipping and transport throughout the nineteenth century world. By 1823, the two men had formally become partners in the business. And 12 years later the firm had grown from being a small shipping company, chartering ships to and from the Iberian peninsula as and when opportunities presented themselves, to one running a regular steamship service under the splendid name 'The Peninsular Steam Navigation Company'.

The first ship regularly plying the Peninsula route for the company was *William Fawcett*, a wooden paddle streamer chartered from The Dublin & London Steam Packet Company. One of its directors was a former Royal Navy officer called Captain Richard Bourne, who met Willcox and Anderson in 1834, and was to play a pivotal role in the P&O story.

The native Dubliner, by now 64, was well-connected and boasted experience both of steam navigation and winning mail contracts. He at once saw the potential of the Peninsula run and set about drawing investors to the company.

Crucially, in 1837, Bourne signed the company's contract with the Admiralty to run a regular mail service from Falmouth to Spain and Portugal, via Vigo, Oporto, Lisbon, Cadiz and Gibraltar. The first contract mail sailing – the 933-ton *Don Juan*, advertised as 'the largest and most powerful ship yet afloat' - departed from Falmouth on 4th September, 1837. Today, this date is accepted as the true foundation of P&O.

Along with *Don Juan*, which was tragically wrecked off Tarifa on the homeward leg of its first journey to the Peninsula, there were four other vessels in that first P&O fleet – *Tagus*, *Braganza*, *Liverpool* and *Iberia*. These ships would become the first of hundreds to fly the now famous P&O flag, which was derived from the company's first routes: blue and white for the Portugese royal house of Braganza and red and gold for the Bourbons of Spain. Anderson and Willcox had shrewdly supported the ruling royals in the respective Portugese and Spanish civil wars, thereby earning

DON'T MISS THE BOAT
GO BY
**P&O**
IT'S MORE COMFORTABLE

**P&O**
LIST OF
PASSENGERS

Above: Captain J.B. Browning and Officers of the *Maloja*, 1930. *(P&O Heritage)*

Right: A promotional card for 1935-6 season and a Passenger list for *Rajputana* dated 15th June 1935. *(P&O Heritage)*

the right to use the coveted colours, in much the same way as the royal warrant-holders of today.

By 1840, P&O had been awarded the contract for the carriage of mails to Britain's empire in the East, so its horizons were expanded beyond the seven-day run to Gibraltar as its ships now sailed across the Mediterranean and down to Alexandria in Egypt, home to the toppled lighthouse which had been one of the seven wonders of the ancient world. The first ship to run the route was the *Oriental*, which carried both passengers and bullion along with the mail.

Fittingly, given the geographical expansion heralded by this new service, the word 'Oriental' was added to the company's name and, on the last day of 1840, the Peninsular and Oriental Steam Navigation Company was incorporated by Royal Charter.

The original Egyptian mail contract had stipulated that a mail service to India should be established within two years. So the company became steadily more 'Oriental', extending its service to India and Ceylon, and later to Singapore, Hong Kong and Australasia.

The passenger experience on P&O in the 1840s bore scant re-semblance to the profusion of relaxing and enjoyable on-board activities which characterise the P&O Ferries fleet of the twenty-first century.

Back then, before the invention of stabilisers for ships, heavy seas would make life aboard highly uncomfortable. It just so happened that most of the company's routes involved traversing the Bay of Biscay, home to some of the most ferocious storms in the Atlantic. Unsurprisingly, few passengers spent much time out on deck.

Decades before the advent of refrigeration on ships, animals had to be shipped alive before being slaughtered for food, making conditions for their human co-travellers less comfortable still.

Nor was discomfort confined to the seas. Until the Suez Canal opened in 1869, the passage to India involved crossing 150 miles

9

**Above: 'For the best at sea sail P&O' poster by Frederick Griffin c.1956.** *(P&O Heritage)*

of desert on the route from Alexandria to Suez and the Red Sea.

A former British Army officer, Lieutenant Thomas Waghorn, had some years previously set-up a courier service over much of the route by camel. At one point, it was estimated that some four thousand camels were carrying mail, luggage and freight to Suez. Passengers were transported by an altogether slower route:

starting with horse-drawn barges on the Mahmoudie Canal, then vermin-ridden steamers down the Nile, and finally in horse-drawn six-seater wagons from Cairo to the coast.

Before long, however, the Egyptian railway from Alexandria had reached Cairo and the novelist Anthony Trollope, employed as a senior official by the Post Office, negotiated with the Egyptian government for the mail to be carried on a new link to Suez.

By the late 1850s, P&O was running weekly mail services to the Peninsula, twice monthly to India and China, and every two

## WHY SAIL ACROSS WHEN YOU CAN CRUISE ACROSS?

P&O Ferries today often sells its services by saying that your holiday begins as soon as you set foot on the ship. This idea – that travel is one of the great adventures which life has to offer and should be enjoyed to the full – is central to the history of P&O.

The essentials came first. Electric light was introduced to the *Chusan* in 1884, swiftly followed by refrigeration, radiators and electric lifts.

By the time the 'Straths' – five ships known as the 'White Sisters' because they were the first to sport the company's new white livery – were introduced to the Australian route in the 1930s, all cabins had running water, with hot and cold in first class.

It was said that there were only six occupations to indulge in for those travelling by sea: 'to eat, drink, sleep, flirt, quarrel or grumble'.Eating came first, of course. In the days prior to refrigeration, what food the ship's purser loaded on setting sail, and what he could pick up at ports visited along the way, was vital to keeping the passengers well-fed.

Over time, dining became a much grander affair, with daily menus printed on board. For gala and fancy dress evenings, specially designed decorative menus were printed, some of which survive and can be seen displayed in the club lounges of the P&O Ferries' ships of today.

Anyone enjoying a good wine on a P&O ferry in 2017 must have some cause to lament not having been on one of the ships 150 or so years earlier. Back then, the company was one of the few lines to supply free drinks – wine, beer and champagne twice a week.

Out on the decks, a profusion of games flourished. Quoits, tugs of war, swimming, sunbathing and ping-pong were enduringly popular. At night, there was dancing to professional bands and cinema shows. Above all, fancy dress retained its popularity, with Bedouins, pirates and explorers all popular costumes.

The much-loved *Canberra*, which served in the Falklands War, pictured here off Spitzbergen, Norway. *(P&O Heritage)*

months to Singapore and Sydney. Eventually, the mail from England would be sent to Marseilles by train where it would be loaded onto a P&O ship arriving from Gibraltar, thereby bypassing the fraught leg of the journey across the Bay of Biscay.

Arthur Anderson would live until 1868 (his partner Brodie Willcox died six years earlier). By then he could look back on a life of remarkable achievement. As well as being chairman of P&O, he had represented the Shetland Islands in the House of Commons as a Liberal MP, and found time for numerous charitable endeavours, including the endowment of the Anderson Educational Institute in his native Lerwick. This establishment would become Anderson High School, whose doors remain open to this day, with 900 pupils currently on its register.

The P&O mail steamer service which Anderson and Willcox pioneered was considered one of the wonders of its age. A regular, reliable service was not only essential for commercial reasons, but also as a lifeline for Britons working overseas, often in the most far-flung reaches of the empire.

For P&O passengers it provided an opportunity to keep in touch with loved ones en route. Well into the twentieth century, letters home were punctuated with the expressed need to break off so that a letter could catch the mail at the next port of call.

# Chapter two

# P&O makes its mark in the twentieth century

The deaths of Wilcox and Anderson saw a new regime at the company's helm and a gradual improvement in P&O's fortunes, which had suffered from competition after the opening of the Suez Canal in 1869. Thomas Sutherland had joined the company as an office boy at the age of 18 and in 1872, at the age of just 38, he took over the role of chairman and remained in this position for an impressive 42 years.

During the early years of the twentieth century, P&O acquired first the Blue Anchor Line and then the British India Steam Navigation Company, which gave it access to further markets throughout South East Asia while the emigrant and cargo trade to Australia blossomed. The 1916 acquisition of the New Zealand Shipping Company and the Federal Steam Navigation Company gave access to New Zealand and the frozen food trade, while further expansion saw markets extended to the West Indies and trading on a worldwide basis. In 1918 P&O acquired a majority shareholding in the Orient Line and two years later Britain's oldest shipping company, the General Steam Navigation Company (GSNC), also came under P&O's wing. By 1923, the company owned 500 ships.

The end of the war in 1945, coupled with the independence of India in 1847, marked the start of a rapid decline in the passenger liner trade to the sub-continent. In response to the changing times and trading patterns, P&O's post-war emphasis was directed towards cargo traffic and the oil tanker trade. The growth of post-war civil aviation eventually brought about the termination of all its liner traffic but not before the introduction of the futuristic looking *Oriana* (1959) and *Canberra* (1960). The year 1961 saw the abolition of national service and the termination of some ships in the British India fleet which had previously been used as troop carriers. Enterprisingly, educational cruises were taken up using some of British India's more modern vessels.

The 1960s proved to be a difficult period for

New P&O Neon Sign being installed at the P&O Head Office at 14-16 Cockspur Street, May 1956. *(P&O Heritage)*

shipping with the slow but inevitable move to containerisation, which P&O helped to pioneer through its membership of Overseas Containers Ltd. From the ferry perspective, 1965 saw the introduction of North Sea Ferries, a joint operation with the Dutch company Royal Nedlloyd, on the Hull–Rotterdam service. The diminutive roll-on roll-off vessels *Norwind* and *Norwave* soon proved their worth by transporting cars (and their passengers), lorries and trailers on nightly passages across the North Sea.

Further changes were to occur during the 1970s and 80s. Rationalisation saw the ending of the old company names that P&O had retained throughout the years and diversification brought about the acquisition of the construction company Bovis. The ending of the traditional liner services came in 1969 and the passenger traffic on which the company was founded now consisted of North Sea Ferries and the growing cruise trade.

> *the roll-on roll-off revolution completely changed the nature of the European ferry industry by promoting the year-round carriage of freight*

Townsend Car Ferries' *Free Enterprise I* at Dover. *(Ken Larwood)*

The start of the transport revolution with loading cars at Calais onto the *Forde*. *(John Hendy collection)*

The shop area on board *Free Enterprise I*. *(Ferry Publications Library)*

The *Viking III* in the Solent. *(Ferry Publications Library)*

Buoyed by its success in the latter sector, in 1974 Princess Cruises was acquired allowing greater access into the lucrative US cruise market. Sitmar Line became part of the P&O portfolio during 1988.

Jeffrey Sterling joined the board of P&O in 1980 and became its chairman three years later. In 1985, a merger between Sterling's own company and P&O introduced numerous non-shipping concerns into the P&O Group, ranging from exhibition centres to tool-makers and a security company. More importantly from the standpoint of this present book, December 1986 saw the acquisition of the European Ferries Group (EFG) whose orange-hulled ships traded as Townsend Thoresen on ferry routes across the English Channel, North Sea and Irish Sea. But EFG was not just about ferries as they too had diversified into ports and US property markets. The tragic loss of the *Herald of Free Enterprise* off Zeebrugge in March 1987 soon saw the renaming and repainting of the ships and the creation of P&O European Ferries.

Further property acquisitions took place during the 1990s along with most of the Ellerman cargo trade, which was purchased from Cunard and which gave P&O total control of the UK–Australasia container trade, in addition to significant shares in the Europe–South Africa market. Major investments in China were also a feature of this period but the construction of the Channel Tunnel saw some 40 per cent of the cross-Channel

Otto Thoresen at Southampton'.*(Ferry Publications Library)*

and planned to sell off its bulk shipping while floating its container business, which was eventually brought by Danish company Maersk in 2005.

In March 2006, the rest of the P&O empire, which was still one of the world's major port operators at the time, was sold to DP World for £3.3 billion. Today, DP World takes great pride in its association with the venerable name of P&O and is committed to the work of P&O Heritage, which exists to preserve and promote the history and collections of P&O.

### P&O FERRIES

P&O Ferries is historically an amalgamation of a number of separate concerns that were later acquired by P&O. Three visionary shipping entrepreneurs were each responsible for founding and developing their own ferry operating companies. Each, quite separate, business was later to grow and flourish under the wing of the European Ferries Group (EFG) before it was acquired by the P&O Group in 1986.

### STUART TOWNSEND

Stuart Townsend started a motorists' service to Calais using a small, chartered, collier at Dover in 1928. Two years later, his

market disappear and bring pressure to bear concerning some sort of rationalisation. If the ferry business was in the doldrums, the cruises sector was booming, which prompted the construction of the world's largest cruise ship, the 108,900 gross ton *Grand Princess*.

A joint venture with the Royal Nedlloyd Group made the new consortium one of the world's largest container shipping companies, while in 1998, in a bid to reduce operating costs by £75 million a year, P&O European Ferries merged its Eastern Channel operations with those of rivals Stena Line and formed P&O Stena Line; an arrangement which was to last for just four years.

As the millennium approached, further restructuring was afoot with much divestment taking place streamlining P&O into four core businesses. In October 2000 it demerged P&O Princess Cruises (which was purchased by the USA's Carnival Corporation in 2003)

Prince Philip at Tilbury Docks during his visit to the port, pictured with Mr F.B. Bolton, Chairman of ASN and Mr M.K. Bustard, Managing Director of the Company. *(Ferry Publications Library)*

On the quayside at Preston, an Evan Cooke's transport lorry prepares to load. *(Ferry Publications Library)*

The Sun Deck on the *Bardic Ferry* with passengers awaiting the evening sailing to Preston from Larne. *(Ferry Publications Library)*

Townsend Bros Car Ferries Ltd converted the redundant First World War minesweeper *Ford* (later renamed *Forde*) and converted her for car ferry operations. Townsend even had the foresight to have a stern door added for possible future use as a drive-on ferry, although lift-on lift-off remained the order of the day. Townsend's service was seasonal and strictly for the benefit of tourists, many of whom wished to visit the battlefields of Flanders and the Somme.

In 1949, Townsend purchased the sale-listed River-class frigate *Halladale,* which, following a major conversion at Cork, took up service to Calais in April 1950. The company was floated on the stock exchange during 1956 and eventually acquired by the Coventry-based Monument Securities Ltd under their chairman, George Nott. Later, led by the energetic Roland Wickenden and then, following his untimely death, by his brother Keith, the company went from strength to strength and became a major force within the British ferry industry. The first of eight 'Free Enterprise' class ferries came in 1962 and three years later a service to Zeebrugge became immensely popular, as the roll-on roll-off revolution completely changed the nature of the British ferry industry by promoting the year-round carriage of freight.

## OTTO THORESEN

Otto Thoresen was a Norwegian ship owner who, in 1964, introduced a pair of bright orange-hulled, multi-purpose car ferries on routes between Southampton and Cherbourg and Le Havre. The nationalised railway company, British Railways, was in the process of withdrawing services from its Hampshire base, operating, as it did, overnight passenger services to Le Havre and St Malo. The railway ships were functional, staid and comfortable but represented an era that was fast disappearing as motorists demanded an up-to-date, brighter and slicker way of crossing the Channel. British Railways saw no future in Southampton and required the two remaining ships for conversion to car ferries at Dover and Newhaven, thereby leaving the door open for Thoresen to exploit.

The *Viking I*, and her identical sister *Viking II*, took the Channel by storm and were the first drive-through cross-Channel ships, introducing modern Scandinavian design and ambience to a tired service. They made an immediate impression and a third vessel was soon ordered, although winter work elsewhere would inevitably be sought for one of the trio as traffic was not then sufficient to keep all three busy at Southampton.

In June 1968, Townsend acquired Thoresen, the European Ferries Group was founded and the combined fleets were in future marketed as Townsend Thoresen. The green-hulled Dover fleet adopted the Thoresen orange in 1976 and for the next ten years was the major force in Channel operations.

## FRANK BUSTARD

Lt. Col. Frank Bustard was responsible for pioneering the first roll-on roll-off service for freight across both the southern North Sea and Irish Sea, and in 1957 introduced the world's first purpose-built ro-ro vessel, the *Bardic Ferry*. Prior to the war, his initial vision was for a cut-price, trans-Atlantic liner service, hence the name of his company: the Atlantic Steam Navigation Company (ASN). But

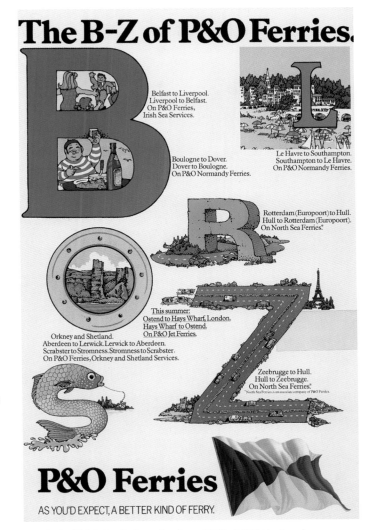

The B-Z of P&O Ferries', poster from 1980. *(P&O Heritage)*.

during the war, when he was given the task of preparing vessels for the D-Day Landings, he saw the tremendous potential of the ro-ro concept on which he was later to capitalise.

In 1946 Bustard was able to lease three war surplus LSTs (Landing Ship [Tank]) from the Royal Navy. Commencing military charters with the *Empire Baltic* in September that year, from Tilbury to Rotterdam and later to Hamburg and Antwerp, this soon

Townsend Thoresen's *European Trader* (FotoFlite).

Normandy Ferries' *Dragon*. (FotoFlite)

developed into a full commercial service. Two years later, a further former LST (renamed *Empire Doric*) was acquired and commenced service between Preston and Larne – the world's first roll-on roll-off commercial service. In 1950 the *Empire Gaelic* started a further crossing of the Irish Sea linking Preston with Belfast.

In April 1954 the ASN was nationalised and was eventually acquired by the European Ferries Group (EFG) in 1971. Following nationalisation the former LSTs were superseded by purpose-built tonnage, although the company's ships retained their ASN livery and on-board standards. In 1965 Tilbury's operations were switched to Felixstowe, which was then a tidal dock on the banks of the Orwell Haven in Suffolk. Its subsequent success story is most certainly attributable to the EFG who saw its potential to become the country's major container port.

Normandy Ferries' n.f. *Tiger* (FotoFlite)

Southern Ferries' *Eagle* (FotoFlite)

The historic link between ASN operations at Felixstowe and Preston (later Cairnryan) meant that they were inevitably connected in a way that other operations of non-ASN heritage were not.

## NORMANDY FERRIES AT DOVER

The long-established Burns & Laird (a P&O subsidiary company) service linking Ardrossan and Belfast was operated by the 1967-built car ferry *Lion*. However, the 'Irish troubles' had understandably caused reluctance to visit the province and the service was subsequently losing money. It was therefore decided to switch the ship to the Dover–Boulogne service and trade as P&O Normandy Ferries. The *Lion* duly took up service in April 1976 and quickly built up trade on the route that British Rail was rapidly abandoning in favour of Dover–Calais. Such was the *Lion's* success that she was soon joined by the six-year-old *nf Tiger* (ex *Kattegat*) in June 1978 and the *nf Panther* (ex *Djursland*) in January 1980. The latter two were sister ships having been built for the Danish company Jydsk Færgefart for internal service between Hundested and Grena.

With larger ferries, boasting greatly improved facilities, entering service for other operators, the P&O trio briefly thrived but were soon outclassed and, although attempts were made to uprate them, their size prevented all but the most basic of improvements from being made. In January 1985 came the surprise announcement that the EFG had purchased P&O Normandy Ferries for £12.5 million. The *Lion* was serving at Southampton at the time of the sale and so did not return to Dover. The '*Tiger*' and '*Panther*' continued and were repainted in Townsend Thoresen's livery until in July and August 1986 they were replaced by the *Free Enterprise V* (from Portsmouth) and the *Free Enterprise IV* (from Cairnryan)

## NORMANDY FERRIES & P&O SOUTHERN FERRIES AT SOUTHAMPTON

Following the closure of the long-established British Railways service to Le Havre in May 1964, the P&O subsidiary company General Steam Navigation Company (GSNC), substituted a limited cargo link. However, following Thoresen's success in 1967, P&O founded Normandy Ferries to commence a joint Anglo-French service linking Southampton and Le Havre. This involved the British-crewed *Dragon*, which commenced the service in June 1967 and, as from May 1968, the French-flagged *Leopard*. The service was originally planned as a freight operation but it was soon

appreciated that it stood a far greater chance of success if passengers were also carried.

Although the joint service traded as Normandy Ferries, the *Dragon* was in fact owned by Southern Ferries, a subsidiary of the GSNC, while the *Leopard* was owned by S.A.G.A. (Societé Anonyme de Gerance et d'Armement). The basic service was extended by offering a weekly crossing from Le Havre to Rosslare (Co. Wexford), which proved so successful that in the following year a second crossing was operated. However, it was soon appreciated that it was not financially viable to run both ships during the winter and so the *Dragon's* accommodation was upgraded in readiness for an off-season 'Sunshine Route' to Lisbon and Casablanca, which started in November 1968. The *Leopard's* accommodation was also improved and during the winter of 1968/69 she offered sailings commencing in Rouen.

In anticipation that the Lisbon and Casablanca sailings would really prove popular, P&O ordered a large new cruise ferry which, after some delays at her French builders, was eventually delivered in May 1971. The *Eagle* extended the basic route network to include Tangier but although the Lisbon service became year-round, the North Africa calls were not so popular. Following the *Eagle's* entry into service Normandy Ferries surprisingly announced that theywould be dropping the Rosslare calls in order to concentrate on their core English Channel link. This move caused great consternation in Ireland and prompted the Irish Continental Line to commence its own service. Losing the Irish calls made sense as it allowed Le Havre services to be increased by 40 per cent, although it was stated that the Irish service was always profitable.

More expansion at Southampton briefly took place when in December 1973 the Scandinavian ferry *Peter Pan* was acquired to operate a 29-hour service to San Sebastian. Renamed *SF Panther* the new link failed to make the impact that had been anticipated and in October 1975 firstly the *Eagle* was withdrawn, followed soon afterwards by the *SF Panther* when both services were closed. After a period of charter work, the '*Panther*' passed to P&O's Orkney & Shetland operations as its *St Clair*.

After periods of industrial unrest, P&O transferred its Le Havre service to Portsmouth during December 1984. The *Dragon* and *Leopard* were included in the January 1985 purchase by the EFG and continued to operate to Le Havre throughout the 1985 season. Improvements were made to their accommodation and their schedules were modified to allow them to run three sailings each day. However, when in spring 1986 it was decided to transfer the twin Felixstowe-based 'Super-Vikings' to Portsmouth in order to replace the former P&O ships, the inevitable strikes broke out on-board the French-flagged *Leopard*. P&O therefore offered to transfer the incoming *Viking Voyager* to French registry for the 1986 season. Meanwhile the *Dragon* was replaced by the *Viking Viscount* and duly became the *Ionic Ferry* at Cairnryan. There she replaced the *Free Enterprise IV* that was required for the Dover–Boulogne service.

## P&O EUROPEAN FERRIES AT DOVER

With the continuing growth of freight traffic, 1980 saw the introduction of three identical 'Spirit' class ferries. With their double deck loading, limited outside deck space and 'neat stow' bow and stern doors, they were unlike anything previously seen on the Channel. Speeds of up to 24 knots enabled five round trips each day to be accomplished and each in turn broke the pier-to-pier vehicle ferry speed record between Dover and Calais. Ever since 1965, all ferries had been fitted with up-and-over bow visors that were raised prior to docking at Calais and Zeebrugge. The 'neat stow' doors of the new trio slid horizontally around the ships' bows and the failure to ensure that these doors were closed contributed to the Zeebrugge ferry disaster in March 1987. P&O had taken over an ailing EFG just three months earlier and lost little time in distancing itself from the manner in which the fleet had been operated. Within weeks the green funnels

Graeme Dunlop, Chairman and Managing Director of P&O European Ferries (1998-2002) on board the *Pride of Dover* at the launch of the partnership of P&O and Disneyland Paris. *(Ferry Publications Library)*

" *No one who travelled on the ships could have failed to be impressed by what they encountered. The company's past was there for all to see and the travelling public was invited to become part of this cultured tradition.* "

emblazoned with a white 'TT' were painted in P&O pale blue complete with house flag, while the legend 'Townsend Thoresen' was removed from the ships' hulls. During October 1987, P&O European Ferries was born and a rather more sombre, 'ship shape and safe' livery was adopted.

The Zeebrugge disaster understandably meant that the entry into service of the next generation of P&O ferries was to be a very low-key affair. The construction of the Channel Tunnel demanded a major response from the ferry industry and in the building of the so-called 'Chunnel Beaters', the European Ferries Group set out to offer a seamless service that would call into question the financial viability of the 'Chunnel'. P&O immediately embraced the concept but took it even further as it stamped its own vision of service on the two new ships. As built, the interiors of the *Pride of Dover* and *Pride of Calais* were rather dull and Germanic, but P&O soon transformed them by refurbishing public spaces with plenty of architectural detail adorned with reminders of the company's heritage and asked the public, 'why sail across when you can cruise across?' No one who travelled on the ships could have failed to be impressed by what they encountered. The company's past was there for all to see and the travelling public was invited to become part of this cultured tradition. An option for a third ship was not taken up but, instead, it was decided to stretch the *Pride of Kent* (ex *Spirit of Free Enterprise*) in order to complement the 'Chunnel Beaters'. The work was completed at Palermo in Sicily during 1992.

Of the remaining 'Free Enterprise' ships, the '*FE VI*

**Pride of Calais** and **Pride of Dover** (FotoFlite)

and 'FE VII' were sent to Bremerhaven to be stretched in June and November 1985. The work did nothing to improve their aesthetic qualities but converted them to double deck loaders capable of accommodating 60, rather than 24, freight units. The work served to solve an immediate problem and saved the delay and expense for building new ships. During their absence from service, the *Free Enterprise V* and the former ASN ship *Gaelic Ferry* deputised on the Zeebrugge link. On the formation of P&O European Ferries in October 1987, the 'FE VI' became the *Pride of Sandwich* while her sister was renamed *Pride of Walmer*. With the axing of the Dover–Zeebrugge passenger service on the final day of 1991, the twins were duly transferred to the Cairnryan–Larne route.

The final two ships of the 'Free Enterprise' fleet (the 'FE V and the 'FE VIII') were retained to operate the Dover–Boulogne route. Renamed the *Pride of Hythe* and *Pride of Canterbury* in 1987, they continued in traffic until January 1993 when the subsidiary link was suddenly axed. The company's thinking was that rather than operate three routes from Dover, it would be in a far stronger position in which to fight the 'Chunnel' by strengthening its position at Calais. The passenger service to Zeebrugge had closed in 1991, but with the EFG then in partnership with the Belgian government's Ostend–Dover line (Regie voor Maritiem Transport), passengers and their vehicles wishing to cross to Belgium could still do so via Ostend.

Freight traffic to Zeebrugge continued to thrive. The service had been operating since 1965 and, as early as 1967, Townsend had introduced the diminutive *Autocarrier* (the former Kent coast summer excursion vessel *Royal Sovereign*), but she was far from ideal for the year-round task with which she was now presented. With space for just 24 freight units the *Autocarrier* struggled at times, although the charter of the Swedish ferry *Stena Danica* did assist matters. Following the *Autocarrier's* sale to Italian owners in 1973, the company now introduced a series of four

dedicated freight ships, each capable of carrying 46 units. The *European Gateway* was the first and was destined for the Felixstowe–Rotterdam service, and was followed by the *European Trader, European Clearway* and the modified *European Enterprise* (later renamed *European Endeavour*) in 1975/76/78.

The three freighters quickly became victims of their own success, and in October 1991 the first of another series of four ships entered service at Dover to replace them. The *European Seaway* could accommodate as many as 124 freight units and was followed into service in 1992 by the *European Pathway* and the *European Highway*. The fourth ship, originally to be named *European Causeway*, was converted on the stocks to become the *Pride of Burgundy* for the Dover–Calais service. She entered service during April 1993 and became P&O's fifth ship, enabling the company to operate a seamless, every 45 minutes, shuttle in which the introduction of club class lounges provided passengers with a degree of excellence that had been missing ever since the days of the fabled 'Golden Arrow' express service.

## A JOINT VENTURE

During 1984, the former British Rail (Sealink) fleet had been denationalised and acquired by the Bermuda-based Sea Containers Inc. Now trading as Sealink British Ferries, the new owners had promised much but had provided very little in the way of new tonnage. Following a protracted hostile take-over bid, in May 1990 the Swedish company Stena Line acquired the business for £259 million. The Swedes quickly sought to stamp their own economies and restructuring on the business, which threw the company into financial turmoil. Following P&O's initiative it also sought to offer a five-ship seamless service and moved to enlarge its local fleet. Whereas the P&O ships were all purpose-built and ideally suited to the Dover–Calais route, Stena now introduced an eclectic group of ships, some of which were far from suitable to the demands of the most intensive ferry route in the world. An inevitable split between Stena and its French partners Société nationale des chemins de fer français (SNCF) occurred in 1996 when the French set up their own operation, SeaFrance. They too moved to enlarge their fleet resulting in overcapacity and reduced profits for all concerned.

P&O European Ferries was always the proven market leader, catering mainly for the upper-end of the passenger market and never failing to remind its public of its history and heritage as the leading British passenger company. Stena's approach in comparison was far more basic, with its intrusive on-board music and fast food outlets. There really was no comparison.

However, with both P&O and Stena feeling the pinch both from the Channel Tunnel and the SeaFrance operation, in a move to make considerable savings, the British Government allowed both concerns to set up a joint venture during November 1997. The agreement also covered the Newhaven–Dieppe and Dover–Zeebrugge routes. P&O would provide eight vessels and Stena five, while voting rights would be 60/40 in P&O's favour. 'P&O Stena Line' replaced the 'Pride of' prefix on each of the P&O passenger vessels, while the *Pride of Bruges* (ex *Pride of Free Enterprise*) was renamed *P&OSL Picardy*.

The former Stena ships were repainted in the P&O style with blue hulls and their *Stena Empereur* was renamed *P&OSL Provence* while the *Stena Fantasia* became the *P&OSL Canterbury*. Much work was carried out on the former Stena ships to try and raise them to P&O's standard and club class lounges and Langan's Brasseries were added.

The Newhaven–Dieppe route succumbed in January 1999 and a technical problem with the freighter *European Pathway* saw the charter of the former Ostend–Dover Line flagship *Prins Filip*, by now renamed *Stena Royal*. The vessel had been laid up at Dunkirk ever since the demise of the Ostend–Ramsgate link in February 1997, but now presented P&O Stena Line with a golden opportunity of further raising standards across its joint fleet. After entering service in a freight capacity on the Zeebrugge link in November 1998 her charter was extended to seven years. An extensive overhaul followed and the ship was introduced onto the Calais link as the *P&OSL Aquitaine* in November 1999. Work was ongoing but her conversion to the shorter route was the first indication of what the public might expect to see from the joint venture. The outcome proved to be somewhere between the two concerns – better than Stena but certainly below the standard one had come to expect from P&O European Ferries. The *Aquitaine* replaced the *P&OSL Picardy* in the fleet; time had moved on and she was now just too small.

The joint venture lasted for just four years and in spring 2002 P&O was invited to purchase Stena's 40 per cent in the new company for £150 million. At the same time, Stena Line would take over P&O's freight operations at Felixstowe and thus improve its North Sea freight operations. The deal was concluded during October 2002.

P&OSL *Canterbury* and P&OSL *Calais* at Dover. *(John Hendy)*

## ZEEBRUGGE CLOSURE

The Zeebrugge freight service was terminated during mid-December 2002. In what was known as 'Operation Darwin', the *European Pathway* had already been sent to Bremerhaven for her major conversion to passenger mode, while the *European Highway* followed on completion of the final Zeebrugge sailing. The first of the series, *European Seaway*, had been transferred to the Calais link but was to see periods out of service and on charter for wind-farm work. The 36-year history of the Belgian route had come full circle but the opening of the Channel Tunnel had seen huge improvements in the continental motorway network and it was now quicker to drive from Zeebrugge to Calais rather than sail by ship. The freeing up of the twin freighters effectively allowed P&O Ferries to upgrade its Dover–Calais fleet. The 'Pathway' became the *Pride of Canterbury* and replaced the former Stena Line vessel, which had briefly become the *PO Canterbury*, while the 'Highway' became the new *Pride of Kent* and replaced the original 'Spirit' class vessel also of that name.

Shortly before Christmas 2004 the last of the former Stena Line ships, *Pride of Provence*, was withdrawn, while the ending of the *Pride of Aquitaine's* charter occurred in May 2006. At £4 million a year, she was always an expensive ship to charter and operate, later passing to LD Lines/DFDS Seaways for whom she continues to operate.

# Chapter three

# Into the modern era

## DP WORLD – NEW INVESTMENT

In March 2006, the P&O Group was acquired by DP World, principally to gain control of the vast assets in its ports portfolio. DP World promised a major investment programme, which was first illustrated by the acquisition of the Spanish ro-ro vessel *El Greco* (ex *Midnight Merchant*) which was renamed *European Endeavour* in support of the *European Seaway's* freight runs on the Dover–Calais link. This she did for two years before a downturn in traffic saw her laid up and then switched to the Liverpool–Dublin route.

Volker Heil, P&O Ferries head of fleet operations, said: "During August 2008, P&O Ferries signed a €360 million contract with Aker Yards in Rauma, Finland (later renamed STX Europe) for the two largest ferries ever to cross the English Channel. For the first time, the company was presented with a clean sheet of paper without any restrictions being imposed by the P&O Group. This ensured that the new ships were designed from scratch for a uniquely specialist trade.

In previous generations, new ships were simply larger versions of what had gone before but a fresh and open-minded approach provided a number of groundbreaking, and even unique, advances in ferry design. Among these is the hull form which, following extensive tank tests, provides a completely new design in water depths of up to 30 metres.

At 213 metres in length, the 47,592 gross ton vessels are the maximum size that the port of Dover can accommodate and the first to be able to manoeuvre under their own power in wind speeds of up to 50 knots, after which the port is closed. The twin lorry decks can accommodate 180 freight units (representing 2,750 lane metres) more than doubling the capacity of the 1987 'Chunnel Beaters' *Pride of Dover* and *Pride of Calais* that they replaced.

A third vehicle deck allows 195 tourist cars to be housed, while on the two decks above this area space is provided for up to 2,000 passengers."

Thus were born the 'Super Spirit' class ships, the *Spirit of Britain* and *Spirit of France*, that entered service in January 2011 and February 2012. The ships are claimed to be the safest and most environmentally friendly vessels in the Channel and with two more ships mooted, P&O Ferries continues to stamp its authority as the market leader in the Eastern Channel.

## P&O EUROPEAN FERRIES AT PORTSMOUTH

At the time when P&O took over the ailing European Ferries Group, the Townsend Thoresen fleet at Portsmouth consisted of all four 'Super-Viking' class ships. They had been built in Denmark in 1975/76, the first two for services from Southampton to Cherbourg and Le Havre and replacing the first generation of former Thoresen ships, while the second pair was destined to serve the Felixstowe–Zeebrugge link.

With Portsmouth becoming the English base for the company's operations in January 1984, an hour shorter crossing time meant that extra sailings were now provided. In December that year it was announced that the *Viking Venturer* and *Viking Valiant* would be 'jumboised' in order to meet the increasing demand for freight space. A second lorry deck would now enable the twins to carry as many as 60 units. They arrived back in service following their conversions during May and July 1986, joining the former Felixstowe twins *Viking Voyager* and *Viking Viscount* that duly allowed the disposal of the former Normandy Ferries vessels *Dragon* and *Leopard*. The stretched 'Super-Vikings' were placed on the Le Havre route while the non-stretched pair was allocated to the Cherbourg crossing.

With P&O European Ferries at the helm as from October 1988, work was put in place to upgrade the passenger accommodation of all four ships and they now received 'Pride of' prefixes: the *Viking Venturer* became the *Pride of Hampshire*, the *Viking Valiant*

*Pride of Dover* (FotoFlite)

The former Olau Line ship **Pride of Le Havre** with her sister were introduced on the Le Havre route in 1993. *(FotoFlite)*

became the *Pride of Le Havre*, the *Viking Viscount* became the *Pride of Winchester* and the *Viking Voyager* became the *Pride of Cherbourg*.

Continued growth in freight traffic saw a number of ro-ro vessels brought in to assist on the Le Havre route, including the former Dover-based *European Trader* and *European Clearway* at a time when P&O was actively looking for replacement tonnage. After failing to acquire Viking Line's *Athena* and *Kalypso* in 1993, the demise of the German-backed Olau Line on the Sheerness–Vlissingen link presented P&O with the opportunity of chartering its redundant *Olau Hollandia* and *Olau Britannia* – two very fine ships with sparkling passenger facilities but not particularly ideal for the carriage of freight. They eventually appeared as the *Pride of*

*Portsmouth* and *Pride of Le Havre* allowing the former Felixstowe 'Super-Vikings' to be sold and cascading the stretched twins to the Cherbourg crossing. The original *Pride of Le Havre* duly became the second named *Pride of Cherbourg*.

Expansion was in the air during April 1993 when P&O started a new service linking Portsmouth with Bilbao using the former Viking Line ferry *Olympia*, which was renamed *Pride of Bilbao*. The new service proved to be extremely successful attracting healthy tourist traffic along with mini-cruise passengers, but although these pleasing figures were a cause of optimism, the chartering of vessels inevitably meant that profits would be marginal. This coupled with a resurgent Brittany Ferries began to cast a shadow over P&O's continued operation in the western Channel sector.

*Viking Voyager* (FotoFlite)

The *Pride of Hampshire* outward bound for Cherbourg (Miles Cowsill)

The *Pride of Cherbourg* (ex *Isle of Innisfree*) arriving at Portsmouth. (Miles Cowsill)

The *Pride of Bilbao* operated the Spanish link from Portsmouth for 17 years. *(Miles Cowsill)*

*The Caen Express* leaving Portsmouth in 2004. *(Miles Cowsill)*

A further charter was arranged when P&O brought in the spare Irish ferry *Isle of Innisfree* for its Cherbourg operation. Although she lacked suitable cabin accommodation, she was introduced to replace the ageing 'Super-Vikings' which were now 27 years old. Renamed *Pride of Cherbourg*, the ship took up station during September 2002.

Further attempts to upgrade the P&O service took place when in 2004 the company introduced the fast ferry *Caen Express* (ex *Max Mols*) on the Portsmouth–Caen link. The service proved to be extremely popular and there were high hopes for its continuation. The InCat craft complimented the *Cherbourg Express* that had operated the Cherbourg service since April 2002.

The *Norwind* and *Norwave* entered service in the mid-sixties on the Hull-Rotterdam service. *(FotoFlite)*

However, at the end of September 2004, it was announced that P&O Ferries was withdrawing from the western Channel, citing heavy financial losses in spite of increased passenger numbers. Efforts were made with Brittany Ferries to continue the Le Havre route but this failed to materialise. The Cherbourg link was duly closed during January 2005 while that to Le Havre succumbed in September that year. Only the *Pride of Bilbao* was spared and continued to operate the Bilbao link until she too was withdrawn at the termination of her charter in October 2010.

The opening of the Channel Tunnel had caused a pull effect on all Channel crossings, attracting traffic towards the short-sea links where road communications were better, waiting times were minimal, crossings were shorter and fares were cheaper. The longer routes all suffered as a result but the operation of a fleet of six chartered vessels and the failure to invest in new tonnage must be seen as contributory factors.

## NORTH SEA FERRIES – 'SLEEPWAY TO EUROPE'

The North Sea Ferries (NSF) success story in many ways mirrors that of Thoresen at Southampton. The long-established Associated Humber Lines (AHL) operated a traditional lift-on lift-off service between Hull and Rotterdam. Their twin unit load vessels also carried a number of cars and up to 80 passengers, but the nationalised company failed to see the route's potential at a time when the nation's thirst for easy access to the Continent was gathering pace. The roll-on roll-off concept appealed not only to the motorist but also to the freight industry, and P&O's Ian Churcher realised that the opportunity existed to launch a revolutionary new link that immediately appealed to a vast catchment area in Scotland, the North and the Midlands who did not necessarily wish to make the lengthy haul to the South Coast ports before crossing to Europe.

Originally, a consortium of six companies was formed to operate the new company (two British, two Dutch and two German) in which the P&O subsidiary, the General Steam Navigation Company, held a 35 per cent stake. Shortly before the start of the new link, the twin British companies merged giving the P&O Group a 45 per cent share in the operation.

During mid-December 1965 the British-flagged *Norwave* entered service on the 197 mile route. With capacity for 249 passengers, 70 cars and 47x12-metre freight vehicles, the new service was an immediate success. The Dutch-flagged sister ship *Norwind* joined the crossing during the following March, allowing North Sea Ferries to operate a nightly sailing in each direction. The first year's operation saw as many as 40,000 motorists using the service, the £12 return fare including dinner, bed and breakfast. Such was the route's popularity that at peak times extra ro-ro vessels were chartered to carry the freight and it soon became

The *Europic Ferry* arrives at Southampton following operations in the Falkland's War. *(Ferry Publications Library)*

The *Norland* represented a huge advance on their predecessors with accommodation for 1,243 passengers. *(FotoFlite)*

The *Pride of Le Havre* leaving Portsmouth. *(Miles Cowsill)*

# THE FALKLANDS WAR AND P&O

When General Galtieri's Argentina invaded the Falklands Islands on 2nd April, 1982, it was inevitable that P&O — with its long history of rallying to the flag during times of war - would have a part to play in the conflict over the British territory 8,000 miles away in the south Atlantic.

The earliest P&O vessels had been built to defend themselves from the nineteenth century pirates who marauded its routes in the Far East. With the start of the Crimean War in 1854, the transportation of British soldiers, horses and equipment was largely carried out on P&O vessels. Florence Nightingale and her first nurses travelled out from Marseilles on P&O's *Vectis*, en route to her base during the war, the Barracks Hospital in Scutari, which is now in modern-day Istanbul.

Two thirds of the P&O Fleet was commandeered by the government in World War 1, with 80 ships ultimately being lost. The single greatest loss of life came with the sinking of the *Persia* on a regular line voyage in the Mediterranean in 1915. Some 335 lives were lost and the survivors, who included the 2nd Baron Montagu of Beaulieu, clung to a lifeboat for thirty hours without food or water before being rescued.

But even this tragedy was eclipsed by the company's experience during the Second World War, when 182 vessels were lost.

When the Thatcher government asked for help in 1982, P&O was quick to answer the call, making five ships available including the flagship *Canberra*. The 27,000 ton *Norland*, the largest British-registered ferry which for the previous eight years had sailed across the North Sea between Hull and Rotterdam, was another of them. She was re-fitted in Portsmouth and sailed for the Falklands along with sixty volunteers from her regular P&O crew, including the ship's master Captain Donald Ellerby, officers and stewards.

After an 11 day journey via Freetown in Sierra Leone, Hull's twin city, the *Norland* took its place in the British Task Force, charged with assisting the first amphibious landings on the disputed islands by the parachute regiment in San

The *Norland* bracketed by bombs in San Carlos water, 24th May 1982. Painted by David Cobb. *(P&O Heritage)*

Carlos Water, which would become known as 'Bomb Alley'.

The Admiralty had decided that the *Norland*'s side doors would be ideal for landing the men of 2 Para in the battle theatre. On the night of 20th May, 1982, the *Norland* became the first merchant ship to enter San Carlos Water, carrying 1,000 paras with blacked-out faces and the landing craft which would take them ashore.

Low-flying, land-based Argentine warplanes made repeated attacks on the British ships. The *Norland* had a close call when two 500lb bombs crashed into the sea a short distance away from her.

One destroyer, HMS *Coventry*, and two frigates, HMS Ardent and HMS *Antelope*, were lost in the battle. But the warships had successfully kept the strike aircraft away from the landing ships, meaning that the first British troops were back on Falkland Islands soil. Within a month, the Argentines surrendered.

With the conflict won, the *Norland* helped to repatriate the defeated Argentine troops back home. Finally, on 1st February, 1983, the P&O ferry returned to her berth at King George Dock in Hull, greeted by a crowd of thousands waving their flags and cheering the returning crew.

The *Norsun* pictured here in the new livery of the company introduced in 1987. *(Ferry Publications Library)*

clear that the twin ships' diminutive size was actually restricting traffic growth and the company now looked to build a second generation of ships.

Constructed in the same Bremerhaven yard as the first pair, the *Norland* (British) and *Norstar* (Dutch) represented a huge advance on their predecessors with accommodation for 1,243 passengers, 500 cars or 139x12-metre freight vehicles. One feature of the NSF service was that as each ship sailed by night, a generous eight hours was allowed to discharge and load the cargo, with access between vehicle decks being via internal lifts. This was in sharp contrast to the thriving operations in the English Channel which demanded minimal turn round times requiring internal ramps and drive-through operations via a bow door.

The *Norland* duly entered service in June 1974 allowing the original *Norwave* to commence a new passenger service to the Belgian port of Zeebrugge, although the freighter *Norcape* had been operating on the link for some 18 months in order to build up

an acceptable freight base. With the appearance of the *Norstar* at Rotterdam during December, the *Norwind* was duly cascaded to the Belgian link.

With Ian Churcher's retirement from NSF in May 1975, he was made Executive Chairman of P&O Ferries. In 1981 the original consortium of six companies in NSF became a 50/50 operation between P&O and the Dutch Royal Nedlloyd Group.

With the Hull–Rotterdam link a ship short, the charter of Viking Line's *Viking 6* was immediately arranged but, being so small, she was an inappropriate substitute until in November the Irish Continental Line's vessel *Saint Patrick II* took up station in her place.

### THE THIRD GENERATION

Costing £40 million, the British *Norsea* was built on the Clyde as the largest, and final, significant British flag passenger ship constructed in Britain since Cunard's *Queen Elizabeth 2* in 1969. The Dutch contribution to the Rotterdam link was the *Norsun*

The **Pride of Rotterdam** undergoing sea trials. *(Ferry Publications Library)*

which was built in Yokohama, Japan. The twins' delivery introduced a new Dutch inspired two-tone blue and white livery while, at the same time, the stretching of the *Norland* and *Norstar* by 20.5 metres would increase their cargo capacity by 20 per cent and allow the revamped Zeebrugge route to further prosper. As with the original pair of North Sea Ferries, the 1974 twins had become victims of their own success and at Zeebrugge a new terminal on the famous Mole was opened in 1984, which allowed for direct access to the open sea without having to negotiate a system of lock gates. Freighters had greatly assisted with the Belgian traffic and during January 1986 the charter of the German twins *Thomas Wehr* and *Gabrielle Wehr* gave the Belgian service 50 per cent more freight capacity.

The *Norsea* and *Norsun* finally entered service in May 1987 allowing the earlier twins to sail to Germany for stretching. Their arrival back in service saw the, by now, hopelessly outdated *Norwave* and *Norwind* sold for further service in Greece. The year 1987 was hailed as a 'landmark year' for North Sea Ferries and also

saw the opening of a new £5 million terminal at the King George V Dock, where all NSF's Hull-based operations were based.

Next to appear on station were a pair of 'super-freighters' built to provide an express, 22 knot, cargo service between a recently built riverside terminal at Hull and a brand new berth at Europoort (Rotterdam). The Dutch built *Norbay* and *Norbank* were the company's answer to the Channel Tunnel which, it was feared, would draw more traffic towards the shortest crossings. More drivers than ever before were now accompanying their lorries and with three freight decks accommodating 156x12-metre trailers, space for as many as 114 drivers was welcomed by the company's freight clientele. The new fast service cut the crossing time by two hours 30 minutes and duly commenced in October 1993, while extra freight ships were chartered to carry excess cargo on the route.

During September 1996, it was announced that the P&O Group had purchased the 50 per cent share in North Sea Ferries from its Dutch partners Royal Nedlloyd for £25.5 million. Along with the

The main restaurant on the *Pride of Rotterdam*. *((Ferry Publications Library)*

The Irish Bar on the *Pride of Rotterdam*. *((Ferry Publications Library)*

company's Felixstowe operations, from the start of 1997 the fleet would in future trade as P&O North Sea Ferries as a result of which the P&O livery would be adopted.

With demand continuing to grow, it came as no surprise when in January 1999 the order was made for a pair of £90 million fourth-generation ferries. Built in Venice for delivery in 2001, the twins represented a complete design change for the Hull–Europoort route. Although their passenger accommodation was not significantly raised, the vast increase in vehicle deck space would in theory allow the new ships to make huge savings by withdrawing the super-freighters *Norbay* and *Norbank,* while operating to the same 22-knot schedule. Three vehicle decks would accommodate 3,400 lane metres for freight in addition to 1,500 lane metres for double-stacked container units and spaces for 250 tourist cars.

The first of the world's largest cruise ferries was the Dutch-crewed *Pride of Rotterdam,* which made her maiden voyage at the end of April 2001. She was followed into service during early December by the British-crewed *Pride of Hull,* which eventually allowed the fleet reorganisation to take place. The third-generation ferries *Norsea* and *Norsun* were duly cascaded to the

> " *The first of the world's largest cruise ferries was the Dutch-crewed Pride of Rotterdam, which made her maiden voyage at the end of April 2001. She was followed into service during early December by the British-crewed Pride of Hull*

Zeebrugge link allowing the earlier *Norstar* and *Norland* to pass to Italian owners. As for the freighters *Norbank* and *Norbay,* the original plan was to switch them to the Felixstowe–Rotterdam link but in January 2002 they were transferred to the Irish Sea. The same year saw the ending of P&O North Sea Ferries, at which time a fleet rebranding took place and the fleet simply became P&O Ferries. During the following January the *Norsun* was renamed *Pride of Bruges* while the *Norsea* was renamed *Pride of York* and at the same time important managerial functions were moved to Dover. During 2011 the Zeebrugge twins were transferred to the Bahamian flag to avoid European employment laws that could impose increased wage costs.

## NORTH SEA FERRIES OVERVIEW

The success of the Hull–Rotterdam link was made possible by introducing four pairs of quite distinct sister ships that were eventually cascaded to the secondary Zeebrugge link. Each new generation quite surpassed the previous one, but it was always necessary to employ extra freight vessels to transport the huge volumes of traffic wishing to use the company's routes. The introduction of the fast super-freighters during 1993/94 allowed a later time of departure without the constraints of using the

The *Norbay* and *Norbank* were built to expand the freight operations on the North Sea. *(FotoFlite)*

King George V Dock. The fourth generation *Pride of Rotterdam* and *Pride of Hull* were intended to accomplish the work of four ships, although at the time of their introduction rival operators were developing their own services from south Humber ports, which deflected some traffic away from the established route.

## FELIXSTOWE

During the troubled post-war period of labour relations that eventually scuttled London's docks, the Suffolk port of Felixstowe took full advantage and was keen to adopt modern working practices. The Atlantic Steam Navigation Company's (ASN) modern fleet of passenger roll-on roll-off vessels had used Tilbury as their

Thoresen Ferries, in October 1974 the former Southampton-based *Viking II* opened a new link between Felixstowe and Zeebrugge. She was joined by the new 'Super-Viking' class ferry, *Viking Valiant*, in January 1974 until such time that the *Viking Voyager* came on station in May 1975 when the '*Valiant*' sailed to take up services at Southampton. With the *Viking Viscount* entering service in May that year, she replaced the smaller *Viking I* which was duly returned to the South Coast.

New tonnage was also forthcoming for the Rotterdam link with the arrival of the *European Gateway*, the first of four similar ro-ro vessels constructed by Schichau Unterweser AG (SUAG) at Bremerhaven (during autumn 1980 she was stretched in order to

Queen Beatrix of Holland on the bridge of the *Pride of Rotterdam*. *(Miles Cowsill)*

The *Pride of Rotterdam* captured at Rotterdam prior to her entry into service. *(Ferry Publications Library)*

principal British base for services to Rotterdam, but in July 1965 the *Gaelic Ferry* was transferred to Felixstowe. Such was the success of the improved link that six months later the Antwerp service followed suit and halved the crossing time from sixteen to eight hours. The final ASN vessel was the *Europic Ferry*, which joined the Rotterdam link in January 1968, but three years later ASN was denationalised and, for £5.5 million, became a part of the European Ferries Group.

Until this time the ASN service was mainly aimed at the freight industry but, now under the wing of an expansionist Townsend

serve the expanding operations on the Irish Sea). In 1976 the European Ferries Group took over the operations and management of the Port of Felixstowe after which expansion quickly followed and involved the construction of a new passenger terminal during 1978. In the previous year the former ASN ships were rebranded and repainted in the bright Townsend Thoresen orange livery.

Other crossings were also tried, namely a passenger link connecting Felixstowe with Rotterdam, but with inconvenient sailing times the link failed to make an impression and was

The *Europic Ferry* leaving the New Waterway. *(Ferry Publications Library).*

How times have changed with freight. A lorry slowly drives aboard the *Cerdic Ferry* . *(Ferry Publications Library)*

The *Cerdic Ferry* at Antwerp terminal. *(Ferry Publications Library)*

dropped. By 1980 Felixstowe had grown to become Britain's busiest container handling port, and such was the growth in lorry traffic that in 1981 the EFG chartered the large 'Searunner' class freight ships *Stena Transporter* and *Merzario Hispania* which, in true ASN fashion, they renamed *Baltic Ferry* and *Nordic Ferry*.

Both ships were requisitioned to join the Falklands Task Force in April 1982 eventually returning to service during the late summer. During their absence the *Syria* and *Hellas*, two more of the 'Searunner' class, were acquired to maintain the Rotterdam (Europoort) link.

While serving in a relief capacity during December 1982 the *European Gateway* was tragically holed, and lost, some 2.5 miles off Harwich, when she was in collision with the train ferry *Speedlink Vanguard*. Within half an hour the 'Gateway' had rolled over onto her side and sank on a shallow sandbank with a loss of six lives. Fortunately 65 passengers and crew were saved and the stricken ship was later raised and sold. The *Europic Ferry* was hastily introduced to maintain the service.

Ever watchful concerning the changing traffic trends within its ferry fleets, the European Ferries Group decided to transfer the 'Super-Viking' class ships, *Viking Voyager* and *Viking Viscount*, to the Portsmouth–Cherbourg link for the summer season 1986. The Europoort freighters *Baltic Ferry* and *Nordic Ferry* were duly converted to passenger/freight vessels by the placing of 650 berth passenger modules on their upper vehicle decks forward of the bridge. Thus the Zeebrugge route's passenger capacity was almost halved but the freight capacity was increased by 30 per cent. Crossings were also reduced from three to two per day, which perhaps indicated the reluctance of motorists to use the Suffolk port, and now that on-board facilities had also been reduced the future of the Zeebrugge link suddenly looked uncertain. The *Syria* and *Hellas* were again chartered, placed in the Europoort link and duly renamed *Doric Ferry* and *Cerdic Ferry*. The ships were eventually purchased outright during 1994.

## P&O TAKE CONTROL

We have already seen that the P&O Group took over the ailing European Ferries Group in December 1986 and, as with elsewhere, the formation of P&O European Ferries during October 1987 saw a change to a rather more sober and 'ship shape' dark blue livery. During 1992, a general renaming policy took place and so the Felixstowe-based ships lost their former ASN names with the

The *Viking II* is seen here on her first arrival at the Belgium port.
*(Ferry Publications Library)*

familiar 'ic' suffixes and became *Pride of Suffolk* (ex *Baltic Ferry*) and *Pride of Flanders* (ex *Nordic Ferry*), while the Rotterdam freight ships became the *European Freeway* (ex *Cerdic Ferry*) and *European Tideway* (ex *Doric Ferry*).

P&O duly sold Felixstowe Docks during 1991 but continued to trade from the port in the same manner as before. Great efforts were made by local management to promote the Zeebrugge link which, in 1994, was marketed as the 'Clipper Line'. Sadly their efforts were in vain and in October 1995 the passenger link was terminated. Both the *Pride of Suffolk* and *Pride of Flanders* subsequently had their passenger modules removed and they were switched to operate with their sisters on the Europoort link. A downgraded Zeebrugge freight link was, however, kept operational by switching the 'Wehr' sisters from Portsmouth. They were replaced in October 1999 by the 75-trailer Swedish ro-ro vessels *Radona* and *Sapphire* that had the advantage of internal ramps, rather than lifts, thus enabling turn round times to be greatly improved.

New Year's Day 1997 saw a major management shake-up involving both North Sea Ferries and P&O Ferries (Felixstowe) Ltd, which would in future trade as P&O North Sea Ferries. Local management was switched to Hull but the twin routes from the

The *Pride of Flanders* showing her passenger module whilst on the Zeebrugge route. *(Ferry Publications Library)*

The *Norstream* arriving at Zeebrugge on her daily run from Tilbury. *(Ferry Publications Library)*

P&O Ferrymasters' *Elk* leaving Gothenburg. *(Ferry Publications Library)*

Suffolk port continued to trade as normal, with the added bonus of the closure of the company's Ipswich operation. However, in 2002 a major overhaul in the company's North Sea operations saw both Felixstowe routes sold to rivals Stena Line as part of a deal which saw P&O take over Stena's 40 per cent share of the Dover–Calais route in a move to become a leaner, fitter company during a period of extremely difficult trading conditions.

After 28 years the Zeebrugge link was closed, in July 2002, while on the 119-mile Europoort crossing the service continued through until September, when the ships and the service moved across the Haven to be based at Harwich.

## OTHER NORTH SEA LINKS

In addition to the company's principal links, a number of purely freight operations involving mainly chartered tonnage have also been a feature of its operations throughout the years.

## TILBURY–ZEEBRUGGE

The most recent route operated by P&O Ferries commenced in July 2007, thereby filling the growing demand from hauliers for a service carrying unaccompanied freight. Tilbury's proximity to the London Orbital Motorway (M25) proved ideal for the 123-mile crossing for which P&O Ferries were quick to exploit an opportunity.

Commencing with the single, small freight vessel *Calibur*, which was capable of accommodating 95 trailers, she was soon joined by the rather larger *Hoburgen* after early indications showed that 100,000 trailers would be shipped each year. Charters came and went with P&O Ferries' own *European Endeavour* and *Norcape* appearing in January and May 2008. More recently, the chartered Bore Line vessels *Norking* and *Norqueen* (both 145 trailers) were cascaded from the Teesport–Zeebrugge route, which were then followed by their successors *Norstream* and *Norsky* (both 185 trailers) and which have maintained the crossing ever since.

## TEESPORT–ZEEBRUGGE & ROTTERDAM

The service linking Teesport and Zeebrugge opened in May 1988, initially using the unsatisfactory French ro-ro vessel *Aquila*. The 268-mile service has used a number of vessels and from 2011 has employed the Finnish flag *Bore Song*, which can accommodate as many as 250 trailers and sails six times a week. She was joined in January 2015 by the *Mistral* (100 trailers) allowing

the company to operate on a daily basis.

The Rotterdam (Europoort) service opened in March 1995 using the Swedish ro-ro vessel *Cupria* (95 trailers) and presently uses the Finnish freighter *Estraden* with capacity for 145 trailers on a three times a week basis.

## IPSWICH–ROTTERDAM

A subsidiary 120-mile link was opened in March 1977 and operated by North Sea Ferries and P&O Ferrymasters. Initially using the chartered *Stena Normandica*, six sailings each week were offered. A number of vessels were chartered to operate the route, which finally closed in April 1995, after P&O Ferrymasters opted to transfer its *Norsky* to the route operated by a further P&O subsidiary, Pandoro, between Liverpool and Dublin and redirect all its traffic to nearby Felixstowe. The navigation of the River Orwell up to Ipswich was always a problem and meant that only vessels of a certain size could be employed.

## TEESPORT–GOTHENBURG/HELSINGBORG

This route was operated by P&O Ferrymasters, which was one of Europe's leading providers of transportation and logistics. In 1977, the acquisition of the *Elk*, which was one of a series of 'Searunner' class freight ships built in South Korea during the late 1970s, allowed the new service to commence. Purchased from Stena Line during 1978 the vessel was later used on the Ipswich–Rotterdam link before joining her sisters *Nordic Ferry* and *Baltic Ferry* in the Falklands Task Force. On her return from the South Atlantic she again took up the Tees–Sweden link on a twice-weekly basis before, in 1999, the *Elk* was transferred to the management of P&O North Sea Ferries and in September ceased carrying the limited number of passengers that had been a feature of her service for many years. In December 2000 the *Elk* was sold to Danish owners and the service was terminated.

## THE IRISH SEA

The P&O involvement in Irish Sea ferry operations stems from two quite separate sources. The North Sea operations of Frank Bustard's Atlantic Steam Navigation Company have previously been discussed and, following his charter of a former LST from the Ministry of War Transport and the commencement of his Tilbury–Rotterdam service in September 1946, the company looked to provide a similar service linking England with Ulster. Refused

The *Ionic Ferry* at Preston. *(Ferry Publications Library)*

permission to operate from Liverpool, Bustard instead opted for the Lancashire port of Preston from where he commenced a service to Larne in May 1948. The *Empire Cedric* initially offered two services each week and in 1950 a further service to Belfast was inaugurated using the *Empire Gaelic*. The impact of the new service was immediate and service schedules were increased to between six and seven each week.

During April 1954, the ASN lost its independence when it was nationalised while during the Suez Crisis, two years later, the entire fleet was sent to the Mediterranean before returning to commercial work in January 1957.

The first of the purpose-built vessels was introduced in September 1957 and based on the design following 11 years' operation with the LSTs. The *Bardic Ferry* entered service at Preston and was soon followed by her sister ship *Ionic Ferry* in May 1958, thereby allowing the 'Bardic' to be transferred to the Tilbury service. A larger pair of twin vessels, the *Cerdic Ferry* and the *Doric Ferry*, came on station at Tilbury in November 1961 and April 1962, after which the original ships were both based at Preston. With four purpose-built ships in operation, the fleet of LSTs was gradually withdrawn with the last of the line, the

*Empire Nordic*, finishing at Preston during December 1966.

A fifth purpose-built ro-ro vessel, the *Gaelic Ferry*, joined the North Sea fleet in March 1964 with its final ship, *Europic Ferry*, entering service in December 1967. The expanding services frequently had to look elsewhere for chartered tonnage during overhaul periods but fortunately Thoresen's 'Viking' ferries were frequently available in the off-peak season. With ASN's de-nationalisation in November 1971, the European Ferries Group acquired the ships, routes and terminals for £5.5 million. Prior to this time, ASN had been looking to transfer its mainland base from Preston to a new port, which they were hoping to develop at Cairnryan in Scotland. The navigation of the River Ribble at Preston caused frequent navigational problems for the larger ships now using the service and this, combined with labour problems at the Lancashire port, hastened the closure of the original link. The EFG soon endorsed the move to Cairnryan and the *Ionic Ferry* opened the new link in July 1973. The Preston–Belfast service continued with the 'Bardic' and 'Doric' before it also was abandoned 12 months later and moved northwards to the short-sea route.

What had essentially been a service for

> *Tilbury's proximity to the London orbital motorway (M25) proved ideal for the 123-mile crossing for which P&O Ferries were quick to exploit an opportunity.*

freight hauliers and their drivers was now expanded by the route's new owners. The 'Ionic' had had her passenger certificate raised from 55 to 219 prior to moving to Cairnryan in the hope of attracting motorists in competition with the rival 'railway' service between nearby Stranraer and Larne. Encouraged by the initial interest in the new service, during the summer peak season of 1974, the *Free Enterprise III* was transferred to the North Channel from service at Dover. This was followed by visits from the *Free Enterprise I* in 1975 and the *Free Enterprise IV* in the following year. Such was the '*FE IV's*' success that she was to remain for a further 10 years.

The freighter *European Gateway* was transferred from Felixstowe in March 1980 and a double-decked linkspan was also constructed at the Scottish port. The vessel was then stretched by 15.7 metres to increase her freight capacity, but was tragically lost while relieving at Felixstowe in December 1981. The *Gaelic Ferry* was moved northwards in her place until the larger *Europic Ferry* was substituted in March 1983.

Further changes were afoot during 1986 when the *Free Enterprise IV* was moved back to Dover and her place was taken by the surplus Portsmouth-based vessel *Dragon,* which duly became the second named *Ionic Ferry*. Her partnership with the *Europic Ferry* lasted until 1992 in which year the stretched Dover–Zeebrugge twins *Pride of Sandwich* (ex *Free Enterprise VI*) and *Pride of Walmer* (ex *Free Enterprise VII*) became available becoming the *Pride of Ailsa* and *Pride of Rathlin*. The last ASN ship,

*Europic Ferry,* was duly downgraded to freight only and unimaginatively renamed *European Freighter.*

The P&O Group took over the European Ferries Group (Townsend Thoresen) in December 1986 and in the following October P&O European Ferries was formed, the ships adopting a new livery and, in the case of the passenger ships nomenclature.

The arrival in service of the £20 million monohull craft, *Jetliner,* in June 1996 saw 60-minute crossings being offered and six sailings each day. She replaced the *Pride of Ailsa* while the former Dover-based freighters *European Endeavour* and *European Trader* were brought north, in September 1995 and February 1996, in order to accommodate the extra lorry traffic on offer.

Although the story of the Cairnryan–Larne route was always going to be hugely successful, its popularity heavily relied on ferries that had been cascaded from other ports. In January 1999 details were announced concerning the construction of a new 21,000 gross ton passenger and freight vessel that would operate the North Channel route at 23-knots, thereby cutting down the crossing time to just 105 minutes. The Japanese-built ship was named *European Causeway* and was destined to replace the last of the former 'Free Enterprise' class ships remaining in service. The switch duly took place in August 2000 with the *Pride of Rathlin* finally bowing out in the following month.

Such was the success of the new ship that the option was taken up for a sister ship. The *European Highlander* entered service in July 2002 and the partnership has since been unbroken.

The *Dragon* was transferred to the Irish Sea operations 1986 and renamed the *Ionic Ferry*. *(Miles Cowsill)*

During April 2000, the fast-craft *Jetliner* was replaced by the *Superstar Express* from Portsmouth and five years later she in turn was replaced by the catamaran *Express*. In addition to the Larne–Cairnryan operations, services to Troon were also operated but these ceased with the termination of the vessel's charter in 2015. The freight service linking the two ports had previously closed in December 2011 following damage to the *Norcape*, which had replaced the smaller *European Mariner* earlier in the year.

PANDORO AND P&O (IRISH SEA)

The names of Coast Lines, the Belfast Steamship Company and Burns & Laird were once familiar within the Irish Sea sphere of operations. All were subsidiaries of the P&O Group and in 1972, looking to expand its road haulage and freight interests, the parent company formed Ferrymasters (Ireland) Ltd and looked to commence a new service linking Fleetwood with Larne. A new ro-ro terminal was constructed at the Lancashire port and in 1974 P&O acquired the new ro-ro vessels *Bison* and *Buffalo* from Stena Line. In December that year they founded Pandoro (an acronym of P AND O RO – i.e. roll-on). The service linked with both Larne and Dublin in a new venture with the British & Irish Steam Packet Company (B&I) and commenced in February 1975 with the *Bison* operating from the Royal Seaforth Dock at Liverpool. Her sister joined the link during the following month.

The 'Irish Troubles' led to the axing of the traditional Burns & Laird Ardrossan–Belfast day-service (using the *Lion*) and the Belfast Steamship Co's overnight Liverpool–Belfast link (operated by the *Ulster Queen* and *Ulster Prince*) in 1976 and 1981. In spite of this, the Pandoro service flourished and at Liverpool a ramp and terminal were built in the north-west Alexandra Dock using the *Union Melbourne* which, once stretched, was renamed the *Puma*. This proved so successful that the *Bison* and *Buffalo* received similar treatment and eventually an extra vehicle deck so that they were extended and expanded almost beyond recognition. Other

The jumboised ferry *Free Enterprise VII* was moved to the Larne operations in 1992 and renamed *Pride of Rathlin*. *(Miles Cowsill)*

The fast ferry *Express* arrives at Cairnryan. *(Gordon Hislip)*

The *European Highlander* entered service on the Larne-Cairnryan service in 2002. *(Miles Cowsill*

Pandoro's *Bison* at Larne pending her morning sailing to Fleetwood. *(Gordon Hislip)*

ro-ro vessels were drafted in the form of the *Ibex*, the *Viking Trader* (renamed *Leopard*) and the *Pointer* which took up the former Burns & Laird link from Ardrossan to Belfast but was later switched to Larne.

The formation of P&O European Ferries in October 1987 did not affect Pandoro, which continued to operate as a stand-alone operation. The service was expanded in 1993 when the former Dover freighter *European Clearway* started operating from Rosslare to Cherbourg. In January 1996, in line with the company's Burns & Laird animal naming policy, she was renamed *Panther*. Then, with the *Merchant Valiant* acquired for the Ardrossan–Larne crossing, she duly became the *Lion*.

All this changed during late 1997 when P&O European Ferries (Irish Sea) was mooted and the entire Pandoro fleet was renamed. Thus the *Bison* became the *European Pioneer*, the *Buffalo* became the *European Leader*, the *Ibex* became the *European Envoy*, the *Leopard* became the *European Navigator*, the *Lion* was renamed *European Highlander*, the *Panther* became the *European Pathfinder* and the *Puma* the *European Seafarer*.

In 2001, Ardrossan was dropped in favour of Troon as the service had become so popular that Ardrossan's port facilities were unable to cope. To coincide with the move, a new £4.5 million terminal

*Such was the success of the new ship that the option was taken up for a sister ship. The European Highlander entered service in July 2002 and the partnership has since been unbroken.*

was constructed for the *European Highlander* which maintained the link. The *European Highlander* was again renamed to free the name for the new ro-pax ferry at Larne and duly became the *European Mariner*.

Although the story of Pandoro and P&O Irish Sea is broadly one of success, it is fair to say that there were also bad times as well as good. In 1999 it was announced that a new £33 million ro-pax vessel had been ordered from Japan to operate the Liverpool–Dublin route. The ship, named *European Ambassador* entered service in January 2001 and allowed the *European Leader* to transfer to the Fleetwood–Larne crossing.

But all was not well at Liverpool where access to fast turn-round riverside berths had been promised but not delivered and which subsequently slowed down the crossing times, frequently making the published schedules unreliable. The situation was a great cause of frustration for P&O who now decided that it would move the *European Ambassador* and *European Envoy* to offer a new service from Mostyn on the River Dee. On paper it seemed like a good move, with excellent road communications and a much shorter crossing time that permitted extra sailings, but its major downfall was the port's lack of water, especially at low tide. The new route duly opened in November 2001 and from the start was plagued with delays and cancellations. In April 2004, the service was moved back to Liverpool.

Beforehand, in 2002, the Hull–Rotterdam super-freighters *Norbank* and *Norbay* had been transferred to the Liverpool–Dublin service and proved to be popular additions to the link, assisting the company with its plans to develop the accompanied car and passenger traffic.

During Spring 2003, it was agreed that P&O would sell its Liverpool–Dublin and Fleetwood–Larne services to the Swedish concern, Stena Line and that the ill-fated Mostyn operation would be closed. However, all did not go according to plan as the Competition Commission refused to allow the sale of the Liverpool services, but the three-year old *European Ambassador* was disposed of (sailing to the Baltic Sea as the *Stena Nordica*) along with the *European Envoy*. Stena's acquisition of the Fleetwood–Larne route lasted until December 2010 after which the route was closed and its elderly ships were sold. A further withdrawal occurred during 2005 with the ending of the Rosslare–Cherbourg freight link.

More recently, in 2011, the second named *European Endeavour*, no longer required at Dover, joined the *Norbank* and *Norbay* on the Liverpool–Dublin route.

## P&O SCOTTISH FERRIES

The links connecting the Scottish mainland to Orkney and Shetland were historically operated by the North of Scotland, Orkney & Shetland Shipping Company (known as the 'North Co'), but in 1961 it was taken over by Coast Lines Ltd, which ten years later was absorbed into the P&O.

The new operators saw that the future lay in ro-ro operation and looked around for suitable ships within their own fleet, considering both the *Lion* (Burns & Laird) and the *Norwave* (North Sea Ferries). Neither of these vessels proved suitable and so an order for a new vessel was given to Aberdeen shipbuilders, who provided the third-named *St Ola* which took up service across the Pentland Firth from Scrabster (Thurso) to Stromness. Long delays at the shipyard were replicated ashore in Orkney, where the ship's new terminal was incomplete, and it was not until February 1975 that the ro-ro link was finally opened.

Attention was now directed at the longer link between Aberdeen and Shetland. Mounting losses on the Southampton–San Sebastian route had seen the withdrawal of the *SF Panther* in 1973,

P&O Scottish Ferries *St Clair* leaves Lerwick (Shetland Islands) for Aberdeen. *(Colin J Smith)*

since which time the ship had been on charter in Norwegian waters. This was the ship that was now earmarked to revive the fortunes of the Lerwick link and renamed *St Clair* (IV), she finally took up services in April 1977.

Meanwhile in October 1975, the old North Co. trading title disappeared and P&O Ferries (Orkney & Shetland) was born, the *St Ola* being the first ship to reappear in the company's preferred pale blue livery.

Extra freight capacity was provided in 1975 with the purchase of the vessel *Helga*, which was named *Rof Beaver* ('Rof' standing for roll-on ferry) and placed on the Leith service.

Seeking to expand the services, in 1986 a second passenger vessel became available to operate the Aberdeen–Stromness–Lerwick and direct Aberdeen–Lerwick links. This was the *nf Panther*, which had been displaced on the Dover–Boulogne route by more suitable tonnage. After a thorough re-fit in Aberdeen, which converted a 'day' vessel to 'overnight' status, the renamed *St Sunniva* (III) commenced service during March 1987 – the 150th year since the foundation of P&O.

New Year's Day 1989 saw the creation of P&O Scottish Ferries and a new ro-ro service to Hanstholm in Denmark, inaugurated using the chartered Italian vessel *Marino Torre* which eventually became the *St Rognvald* (IV), replacing the smaller *St Magnus* in service.

Larger tonnage for the Aberdeen–Lerwick route was acquired during 1991 in the form of the redundant Brittany Ferries vessel *Tregastel*, while the Finnish ship *Eckero* was purchased for the Pentland Firth services. After thorough refits in order to upgrade them for their new services, 1992 saw the entry into service of the new *St Clair* which became the largest ship in the fleet. She was followed by a new *St Ola* (IV) which greatly improved the situation on the direct Orkney link.

During the peak season of 1993, the new *St Clair* was tried on a series of sailings linking Lerwick to the Norwegian port of Bergen. This was continued for the following three years until such time that the pressures of the Shetland service demanded that she remain there on a full-time basis.

When, during 1995, the Scottish Office invited companies to tender for a new contract to serve the Northern Isles, P&O Scottish Ferries was successful. However, with new Safety of Life at Sea (SOLAS) directives coming into force, P&O found itself in a difficult position as none of its ageing vessels complied with the demands of the new regulations. With devolution in Scotland on the horizon, shipping operators now looked towards the next round of tendering which took place during March 2000. Four companies all made their bids for the new contract with P&O offering to build new ships to replace its second-hand tonnage. During October it was announced that Clyde and Western Isles operators Caledonian MacBrayne, in partnership with the Royal Bank of Scotland, had been awarded the contract and that the new operation would commence in 2002.

For P&O it was the end of a long history of serving the Northern Isles with the *St Clair*, *St Sunniva* and the *St Ola* all terminating their services in September 2002.

## P&O FERRIES TODAY

With five passenger and eight freight routes operating in the North Sea, Irish Sea and Dover Strait, the P&O Ferries of today is a smaller but fitter and leaner operation when compared to that seen some 25 years ago. In addition, the purely freight operations at Teesport and Tilbury provide hauliers with popular and quieter alternatives to the Low Countries and their busy industrial hinterlands.

Part of P&O Ferries' present success is that the ports from which its ships operate are all on, or

**P&O Ferries warehouse at Whitfield which supplies all the ports of the company 24 hours a day.** *(P&O Ferries)*

adjacent to, good road networks that enable traffic speedy access to its ships that, in turn, serve as motorway extensions and vital links to the holiday destinations and key trading markets. ASN's claim that it was offering its clientele a service which was 'By Road Across The Sea' has never been truer.

Traditional English Channel, North Sea and Irish Sea ferry services were determined by the Victorian railway companies anxious to provide links from their ports and thus extend their spheres of influence overseas. But a port that might have once been ideally sited at the end of a railway line is not necessarily placed at the ideal point for a motorway link.

Of the ports themselves, deep sheltered water with clear access to the open sea, minimum turn round times and efficient shore-side cargo handling is essential. In order to achieve prompt and systematic connections, purpose-built ships with good port fit, adequate bow thrusters to aid manoeuvrability and vehicle decks of sufficient space and size are vital. The high standards of passenger accommodation to suit all tastes and offering a range of retail outlets, restaurants with areas for relaxation both inside and out are also essential. Finally there is the comfort of knowing that with the name P&O, passengers are travelling with Great Britain's oldest and most respected shipping company.

*" Part of P&O Ferries' present success is that the ports from which the ships operate are all on, or adjacent to, good road networks. "*

# Chapter four

# The holiday begins when you set foot on the ship

The creation of P&O European Ferries in October 1987 precipitated the start of a dominant era for P&O in the British–Europe passenger ferry market. The challenge at that time was immense. Faced with the prospect of the construction and opening of the Channel Tunnel, the short-sea routes went through a process of reinvention to make them fit and ready to face the new competitor. This was no cosmetic exercise, but a wholesale revolution, overhauling every aspect of the company and its operations. Three decades on, and P&O Ferries has sustained industry and market leadership, recently moving up a gear to beat off a succession of unprecedented external threats to the business. Whether competing on the short-sea sector, connecting the North of England and Scotland with the Continent, or providing vital links across the Irish Sea, the distinctive and leading P&O Ferries brand remains synonymous with excellence and quality.

How does P&O Ferries continue to thrive on these challenges?

In 1987 the birth of P&O European Ferries combined the heritage, culture and quality of P&O with the strong commercial presence of European Ferries on the short-sea routes. There was an immediate imperative to tighten operating procedures, but the impending challenge of the Channel Tunnel – striking at the heart of the company's business – prompted a wider review of company culture and philosophy. The lengthy construction period for the tunnel gave time to initiate and deliver a complete overhaul of the business.

Recognising that the competitor's offer was going to be utilitarian at best – summed up memorably at the time by sales & marketing director Brian Langford as comprising 'a loo and a light bulb' – P&O European Ferries invested heavily in the fleet. By focusing on the perceived strengths of the ferry product, the company was able to provide a contrasting modern alternative to the tunnel. The cross-Channel experience was positioned as one component of a longer end-to-end journey, which enabled the

company to build on P&O's cruising heritage and distinguish itself by offering an opportunity to relax, take in the sea views, stretch the legs, enjoy a quality meal and catch up on some shopping. None of this, of course, could be offered by the tunnel during the parallel journey. But slick operational delivery was also needed to obviate any possible strengths of the tunnel.

Sister ships *Pride of Dover* and *Pride of Calais* entered service in 1987 with capacity for 2,290 passengers and 650 cars, radically raising the standards and product offer between Dover and Calais. Designed specifically for the route, the vessels incorporated rapid multi-deck loading and discharge and an unprecedented range of on-board facilities, including club class lounges, Langan's Brasserie restaurant, an international food court, offshore shopping, Silverstone's Sports Bar, the Harbour Coffee Company, multiple lounges and an amusement arcade.

At Dover and Calais, P&O European Ferries worked with the port authorities to sharpen up the port operations to provide slick boarding and discharge from the vessels. Backed by high-profile advertising and marketing, the fleet truly lived up to the campaign strapline '*Why sail across when you can cruise across?*'

In a further statement of confidence, £235 million was invested in five superferries between 1991 and 1993; *European Highway*, *European Pathway* and *European Seaway* provided a dedicated freight link between Dover and Zeebrugge, releasing space on the Dover–Calais fleet for passenger business. *Pride of Kent* was refurbished and lengthened by 31.5 metres, and the arrival in 1993 of new-build *Pride of Burgundy* supplemented the *Pride of Bruges* to establish a core five-fleet for the short-sea route. The comprehensive strategy to offer a 'Chunnel beater' service was therefore in place well before the opening of the tunnel, enabling P&O European Ferries to establish itself as the clear market leader for cross-Channel travel, and the company was able to sustain its dominance in the following years.

The opening of the Channel Tunnel in 1994 proved to be just

Tourists experience the sea air and spectacular views long associated with travelling on a P&O ferry.

*Spirit of France* (FotoFlite)

one of a succession of challenges that threatened the stability of the ferry industry.

The traditional ferry business model had embraced significant income and profit contribution from the on-board sale of duty-free products. The substantial savings on offer attracted a large volume of passengers, particularly for day trips and short breaks; this in turn kept fares low and enticed travellers with attractive on-board pricing.

But in July 1999 the opportunity to offer duty-free products ended within the European Union. This, coupled with the initial impact of competition from the tunnel, precipitated the short-term merger of P&O European Ferries services with Stena Line under the 'P&O Stena Line' banner between 1999 and 2002. Further consolidation of services saw the company re-emerge independently as P&O Ferries, with short-sea services concentrated on the Dover–Calais route, having absorbed the former Stena fleet.

The first low-cost flights between Britain and Europe took off in 1996 and a decade of rapid growth followed. This slowed after 11th September 2001, and despite some recovery the low-cost market has been stagnant over the last seven years. The initial flurry of new routes and low fares matured and the range of new destinations capable of driving higher levels of growth, narrowed. The overall market increased, but has now plateaued at this higher level.

P&O Ferries' answer was to meet these challenges head on through investment in a new generation of market-leading vessels, designed to contrast with the inherent weaknesses in their competitors' products. At 47,500 gross tons and 210 metres long, *Spirit of Britain* and *Spirit of France* are the largest vessels operating in the English Channel, almost double the size of their predecessors. This order reflected the clear ambition of consolidating P&O Ferries' market leadership on the short-sea route.

In true P&O customer-focused style, the new vessels were designed from scratch after an extensive consultation process. After sourcing opinions of a multitude of groups, ranging from officers and crew to truck drivers and the many diverse passenger groups who would have an interest in the ships' future operation, a 'Designed for you ... Built for you' philosophy was developed to underpin the design. The completed vessels therefore perfectly reflect the characteristics of the short-sea crossing experience, from the need to be able to find a broad range of facilities quickly, to the ability to enjoy the 'wow' factor of the White Cliffs of Dover

Top: Winners and directors at the annual P&O Ferries employee awards in Maidstone, November 2016.

Left & above: On board the *Spirit of Britain*.

**Double Olympic champion Dame Kelly Holmes (fourth from left) poses with members of the crew of the Spirit of Britain at the ship's launch in March 2011.**

from the open decks or from interior picture windows. Strong P&O Ferries branding and incorporation of the corporate flag palette in interior design pays homage to the group's heritage.

The new sisters were the first passenger vessels in the world to comply with the SOLAS 'Safe return to port' requirements. A hydrodynamic hull design and efficient propulsion systems deliver similar fuel economy to their predecessors, but with dramatically reduced $CO_2$ emissions.

The *Spirit of Britain* entered service between Dover and Calais on 21st January 2011, with *Spirit of France* following on 9th February 2012, permitting the subsequent withdrawal of *Pride of*

*Dover* and *Pride of Calais*.

This vote of confidence in the strengths of the ferry product offered a highly credible quality alternative to airline mayhem and the utilitarian nature of the tunnel.

Pascal Devaux, P&O Ferries' head of port in Calais, said, "The advantages of taking the ferry are enduring, but service quality improvements enhance these further. Packing the car with everything needed to enjoy the holiday, taking advantage of convenient and good road access to and from ports, having the freedom to choose from a wide range of crossing times and

The view from Cote d'Argent restaurant in Calais. Serving superb food cooked by a chef who lives above the establishment, visitors from across the Channel enjoy the sight of P&O Ferries' ships punctuating the panoramic view.

prices, and the ability to take a break from driving and arrive refreshed for the next leg of the journey; all are timeless advantages that position the practicality, flexibility and enjoyment of the ferry crossing well ahead of any alternative. A fresh generation of passengers are now discovering the joys of holiday freedom opened up by P&O Ferries' Dover–Calais route."

The strong emphasis on meeting passenger needs that is apparent on the short-sea route is also reflected in other services across the P&O Ferries group. As the only ferry company in Europe with routes across both the English Channel and the Irish Sea, how does P&O Ferries differentiate itself from the competition?

Michaela Murphy, P&O Ferries' head of customer experience, said: "The on-board offer is designed to appeal to all palates: the brasserie offers a dining experience with waiter service presenting everything from a full cooked breakfast to a light bite or a three course dinner; the food court is all about hearty, traditional family favourites, such as fish and chips, curry or lighter snacks, sandwiches and other chilled options, while a range of bars and cafes completes the portfolio. On the Hull–Zeebrugge/Rotterdam routes there are options to pre-book meals in advance of travel during the booking process. Passengers rightly expect their food to be quality assured, and

P&O Ferries delivers this in the on-board kitchens. Meat is sourced from a master butcher using the AHDB quality standard, which sources the highest levels of independently-inspected quality assurance for meat in England – so, for example, the fillet and sirloin in the brasserie is sourced from Northamptonshire. Fish comes from sustainably sourced waters such as the North Atlantic, while sausages are sourced using farm-assured English pork, and eggs are British Lion Marked free-range. And the range of Starbucks coffees and PG teas are Fairtrade or Rainforest Alliance certified.

Local companies are especially highly valued,, including Kent Crisps (produced from potatoes grown near Ramsgate), Shepherd Neame (whose ales such as Spitfire, Bishop's Finger and IPA are brewed in Faversham), the Belgian Paljas blond beer and IPA (both brewed in Zeebrugge), and Three Choirs dry white wine, an English wine from Gloucestershire."

## NORTH SEA

In 1996 P&O Ferries bought out the 50 per cent stake held by Royal Nedlloyd Group in the North Sea Ferries operation, and the company was rebranded as P&O North Sea Ferries. Continued growth on the routes from Hull to Rotterdam and Zeebrugge enabled P&O to order two 60,000 ton superferries – *Pride of Hull* and *Pride of Rotterdam* – from Fincantieri for the Hull–Rotterdam route.

## MINI-CRUISING WITH P&O FERRIES

In 2016, P&O Ferries said that it would be marketing mini-cruises to Amsterdam and Bruges on its North Sea routes, which are serviced by some of the biggest ships working as ferries in Europe.

Janette Bell, P&O Ferries' managing director, said: "Our North Sea ferries recall the unforgettable style of the famous P&O liners of the past, with first class restaurants, bars and live entertainment."

And what a past those famous P&O liners had, providing memorable experiences to some of the most famous names of their day.

The novelist William Makepeace Thackeray, three years before he published his most famous work *Vanity Fair*, sailed from London to Cairo as a guest of P&O in 1844. He wrote of his tour: "It was one so easy, so charming and I think profitable – it leaves such a store of pleasant recollections for after days, and creates so many new sources of interest – that I can't but recommend all persons who have time and means to make a similar journey...to see the living people and their cities, and the aspect of Nature, along the famous shores of the Mediterranean."

Thackeray's fellow writers, Charles Dickens and Wilkie Collins, were among the other luminaries who travelled with P&O.

By the end of World War Two, the concept of the cruise became more important to the company, as it was faced with a rapidly disbanding empire and competition from air travel.

Then as now, the role of P&O was to bring a hitherto rarefied experience within reach of millions of people. It was the dawn of the new era of leisure travel, of which P&O Ferries is at the forefront to this day.

P&O Ferries has long been active in the communities close to its ports. Here Steve Loram, acting sous chef on the English Channel's *Pride of Burgundy*, presents a prize to the winner of a school Bake-Off competition in Dover in October, 2016. *(P&O Ferries)*

The North Sea services are a very different proposition from other routes in the portfolio. The leisurely overnight crossing provides a strategic link from the North of England and Scotland to the Continent, avoiding the long drive south and making productive use of driver (and family!) rest time. They are another example of the investment confidence and market understanding of P&O Ferries providing the right fleet to meet route demand, matching high capacity to quality on-board facilities.

Terry Chinn, P&O Ferries' operational excellence manager for the North Sea, said: "All Hull–Rotterdam and Hull–Zeebrugge tickets include a standard cabin with lavatory and shower room, towels, bed linen and storage space, with the option to upgrade to an outside, Premier or Club cabin with extra space. Club Cabins also come with colour television and tea and coffee making facilities. There are also a limited number of disabled cabins for wheelchairs users.

As befitting an overnight crossing, there's entertainment to suit all tastes, from those wishing to party the night away to those who want to simply relax and unwind. The Show Lounge showcases live bands, singers and cabaret throughout the evening, while other facilities include a disco, bars and an on-board casino. Others can choose to relax and be entertained by the on-board pianist, or spend the evening watching the latest films in the on-board cinema. The aim is to ensure that the journey is as enjoyable as the destination.

These facilities also enable P&O Ferries to offer a range of minicruises, giving a taste of the on-board cruise experience, packaged with an onward visit to Amsterdam, Bruges, Rotterdam or Ypres.

Overnight crossings on the North Sea eliminate a substantial amount of driving, and travelling while asleep makes the journey more efficient and appear shorter. Yet there's still time to enjoy the on-board facilities, which makes the journey feel

In 2016, P&O Ferries introduced new uniforms for its on-board crew which evoke the timeless essence of the brand, complete with shirts and blouses that sport a Bengal stripe dating back to the P&O service to India in the 1800s. *(P&O Ferries)*

An officer on the bridge of a P&O Ferries ship. *(P&O Ferries)*

P&O Ferries' apprentices at the National Maritime Training Centre. *(P&O Ferries)*

an enjoyable component of the holiday. For families, the excitement of boarding ship, stretching the legs, exploring and getting an appropriate rest sets up the safe onward journey on arrival. And of course, everything needed during the crossing is readily available in the car. For coach and freight drivers there's the additional advantage of a statutory rest period that makes optimal use of the sailing while cutting the driving time to the Continent."

## CAIRNRYAN–LARNE

The journey between Scotland and Northern Ireland is one where speed is of the essence – more of a commuter journey than an opportunity for a cruise experience. So P&O Ferries offers up to seven sailings a day on the fastest and shortest crossing between Cairnryan and Larne, providing exactly what passengers need.

The bespoke-designed *European Causeway* entered service on the Cairnryan–Larne route in 2000 and has operated exclusively on this vital link ever since. Smaller sister *European Highlander* joined

her in 2002. The *European Highlander* is six metres longer than the *European Causeway* and with a top speed of 23 knots is one of the fastest ferries on the Irish Sea. Both vessels benefitted from customer-driven investment in 2013, and now feature more comfortable seating areas, refurbished restaurants, a new menu and an all-new club lounge for those who want a little extra luxury on-board. In the process of continuous development, further improvements were made to the ships in 2016.

## LIVERPOOL–DUBLIN

P&O Ferries' Liverpool–Dublin crossing between England and Ireland is the only passenger service operating between the two countries. With crossing durations from seven hours 30 minutes, the route is scheduled to run around 17 times per week. The service operates from Bootle direct to the heart of Dublin and passengers can enjoy two meals included within the price of the crossing.

The fleet comprises three vessels, and while this is primarily a

The P&O Ferries company choir, which consists of employees from the ships and ports in Dover and Calais, was formed as part of the BBC programme 'The Choir: Sing While You Work' in 2013.  They won the title 'Best Workplace Choir' and are here pictured at a Christmas concert in Dover. *(P&O Ferries)*

freight route, P&O Ferries optimises the accommodation available to offer a popular car passenger service. Sister ships *Norbank* and *Norbay* were built in the Netherlands in 1993 and 1994 respectively, and originally operated on the Hull–Rotterdam route. *Norbank* transferred to the Irish Sea in 2002, with her sister following five years later. Spanish-built in 1997, the *European Endeavour* sailed on her maiden voyage in 2000, entering service for P&O Ferries on the Irish Sea in 2007.

## MARKET LEADERS

P&O Ferries' sustained market leadership across a range of routes is no coincidence. The position has been built and maintained by customer-focused strategic investment, coupled with a relentless drive to deliver quality products, bespoke to individual markets. The pay-off is clear in record recent-era passenger carryings. Despite the challenges posed by migrants and competitor industrial action, the business remains popular and healthy.

*Eastern Docks, Dover* (Maritime Photographic)

# Chapter five

# Over sea and land –
## Development of P&O Ferries freight business

There have been many challenges to the British ferry industry over the last couple of decades. Yet P&O Ferries has, uniquely within the industry, retained its strong position in the key short-sea, North Sea and Irish Sea freight markets, while cementing its status as one of Europe's leading ferry operators.

Over 40 years of cross-Channel freight experience is underpinned by a wealth of expertise, inherent reliability and a commitment to the widely respected P&O Ferries brand.

**Henrik Pedersen, P&O Ferries director of freight sales, said:** "In 2015 P&O Ferries carried more freight between Dover and Calais than in any previous year in its recent history – a 22 per cent year-on-year increase. Both the third and fourth quarters set new records for freight volumes, and freight carryings have now grown to comprise around two thirds of the company's business.

On the Hull–Rotterdam route, P&O Ferries was able to record an 11 per cent year-on-year increase in the number of HGVs carried in 2015. This represented an additional 100 extra vehicles each week, contributing to a total of 52,000 HGVs shipped. The Tilbury–Zeebrugge route also carried record volumes of freight units in 2015, and the new partnership with SOL Continent Line sees growing business between Britain and Gothenburg via Zeebrugge."

How does the company continue to sustain this leading role?

P&O Ferries has a long history of servicing the key continental ports with the best connections to Europe. The services to Rotterdam, Zeebrugge and Calais each demonstrate how a carefully crafted and customer-focused geographical strategy, coupled with a full understanding of the components of customers' businesses, can deliver continued success. Each route is developing innovative solutions for customers, particularly in looking for opportunities to support them in implementing efficiencies and delivering environmental benefits.

Part of the answer also lies in taking a broad view of the crossing as just one element of a much longer journey for the freight haulier. Seen from this perspective, the ferry crossing is advantageous, exploiting the inherent weaknesses of other forms of transit. P&O Ferries now sees itself as a ferry and logistics company, with integrated road and rail links to the continent.

For a journey that originates in Eastern Europe, Italy or the Iberian peninsula, the sea crossing is a small proportion of the overall journey length. Freight drivers are an expensive commodity, constrained by obligatory working-hour regulations, and there are increasing environmental concerns for long-distance flows. If the time associated with the sea crossing can be utilised to satisfy a driver rest period – or be undertaken with no driver at all – then this transit can be turned to productive use.

A review of the routes served by P&O Ferries demonstrates how this strategy is being enacted.

### HULL/TEESPORT–ROTTERDAM EUROPOORT

P&O Ferries offers daily overnight sailings between Hull and Rotterdam Europoort utilising the passenger ferries *Pride of Hull* and the *Pride of Rotterdam*, and six sailings per week to Teesport using the freight vessel *Estraden*.

Rotterdam is Europe's best-connected gateway and hub, with easy road access to all major European industrial centres and a market of 500 million consumers within a 24-hour reach. Road transport is generally the fastest choice for short distances in close proximity to and from the port. Forty per cent of goods leaving the port by road remain in the Rotterdam region, with half destined for the Dutch market and just 10 per cent crossing the border.

Rail transport is also a key component of the modal connections to Rotterdam, with the German border just three hours away via the Betuwe route – a 160-kilometre dedicated route for freight, connecting the Maasvlakte and the port of Rotterdam

directly to the German railway network. Consequently many European destinations can be reached within a day. More than 250 intermodal rail services serve Rotterdam each week, particularly for container traffic, dry bulk cargo, general cargo and chemical products. The Rail Service Center Rotterdam (RSC), located in the port of Rotterdam, handles shuttle trains and combined transport.

P&O Ferries' terminal at Rotterdam Europoort has benefitted from a 250-metre rail siding extension that has equipped it to handle longer freight trains from Central and Eastern Europe, significantly enhancing capacity and efficiency. The loading and discharge times at both Hull and Rotterdam Europoort are now among the fastest in the sector.

Both Hull and Rotterdam Europoort offer container handling facilities and the vessels have seven-metre deck heights that enable double-stack capability and the shipment of a wide range of unaccompanied units. The crossing time of 11 hours, coupled with dedicated cabin accommodation and facilities on board for commercial drivers, enables them to take advantage of the statutory rest period while travelling between the two ports.

## HULL/TEESPORT–ZEEBRUGGE

P&O Ferries serves Zeebrugge by offering up to ten sailings each week on the Tilbury service using the dedicated freighters *Norsky* and *Norstream*, a daily overnight sailing to and from Hull with the multi-purpose vessels *Pride of Bruges* and *Pride of York*, and 12 sailings per week to Teesport with the freighters *Boresong* and *Mistral*.

Nick Pank, P&O Ferries' head of sales on the North Sea, said::"In Zeebrugge, road remains the dominant method of transport to and from the port, but rail forms an increasingly important connection. It is particularly attractive for container traffic, paper and new cars, which are transported by block trains. As with Rotterdam, the port benefits from onward

**P&O Ferrymaster containers being loaded on freight wagons at Zeebrugge.** *(P&O Ferries)*

P&O Ferrymasters' tug driver loades another unit onto the *Pride of Bruges* at Zeebrugge. *(P&O Ferries)*

international maritime connections from both container and ferry services.

The port is also served by the European inland waterway network utilising estuarial vessels. The shift of cargo from road to both rail and inland navigation is a key policy priority, to optimise transit in an environmentally friendly fashion. Zeebrugge is a leading railway port with direct connections into the terminals and 16 per cent of all traffic utilising rail – 40 per cent of container traffic reaches the hinterland by rail. Around 131 weekly trains were scheduled in 2016, to connect Zeebrugge to Austria, Germany, Greece, France, Italy, Poland, Romania and Spain. An ambitious investment programme, which will deliver an additional track between Zeebrugge and Bruges, commenced in March 2016, complementing the installation of an additional double track between Bruges and Ghent and an extension of the port rail marshalling yards.

P&O Ferries now has a groundbreaking partnership with Swedish-based SOL Continent Line that enables North Sea customers to ship freight to the company's hub in Zeebrugge for onward connections to Scandinavia via SOL's Zeebrugge to Gothenburg service. Since the service began in 2015, P&O Ferries has shipped over 2,000 freight units in both directions between Gothenburg and Teesport, and Tilbury and Hull."

The partnership with SOL Line simplifies the booking process, with customers making a single call to arrange for shipment between Scandinavia and Britain. Already this is proving popular with Scottish drinks manufacturers who need to transport large volumes of whisky to the highly lucrative Swedish and Norwegian markets. P&O Ferries expect to conclude more partnerships in the future to further extend its geographical reach.

The Port of Hull. *(Ferry Publications Library)*

## TILBURY–ZEEBRUGGE

P&O Ferries Tilbury–Zeebrugge route carried record volumes of freight units in 2015, continuing a track record of continuous growth since the service first operated in 2008. Volumes have tripled over this period, and the service now nears maximum capacity.

Tilbury has strong geographical advantages for hauliers, being just 25 miles from Central London and seven miles from the M25. The route offered 22 weekly departures in 2016, with two dedicated vessels, *Norsky* and *Norstream*, capable of carrying double-stack containers, while also offering cabins for accompanied freight drivers.

Proximity to London opens up a huge market for hauliers and the route's success has been built on the import of consumables such as paper, steel, food, detergents and machinery, where there is a desire to get products as close to the capital as possible. The import of unaccompanied new cars from Europe is also a growing trade, with 35,000 units shipped from one manufacturer in 2015 alone. Add to this the growth in volume of regular shipments of hazardous goods attracted by a freight-only route and the prospects for the Tilbury–Zeebrugge service look sound.

## DOVER–CALAIS

Short-sea services have long sustained the largest volume of business, but also face the heaviest competition. The multi-purpose vessels *Spirit of Britain*, *Spirit of France*, *Pride of Burgundy*, *Pride of Canterbury* and *Pride of Kent* maintained an intensive service across the Dover Straits. The addition of the freighter *European Seaway* with the capability of making four round-trip crossings daily from August 2015 brought capacity for 120 freight vehicles on each crossing. The combined six-ship fleet now offers up to 58 daily sailings, enabling a record of 1,340,317 freight units across the Channel in 2015.

In contrast, the volume of through-rail traffic taking the Channel Tunnel has consistently fallen well short of Eurotunnel projections. The vehicle size restrictions of the British 'loading gauge' relative to the continental network, the requirement for a change of traction on entering or leaving France, coupled with the migrant crisis has inhibited service growth. Volumes fell to 2,421 freight trains in 2015 – or an average of three daily services in each direction – and Eurotunnel has now informed the European Commission that the joint objective of 5,000 rail freight trains by 2018 cannot be achieved if the current migrant situation persists. So how can P&O Ferries tap into this underperforming rail market?

Step in P&O Ferries' new agreement with VIIA – the 'rolling motorway' logistics subsidiary of SNCF – to provide cross-Channel transportation for unaccompanied freight trailers in conjunction with the VIIA Britanica intermodal rail service.

Stephen Weaver, P&O Ferries head of commercial strategy and new business development, said: "This opened on 29th March 2016, with the first train of unaccompanied road trailers leaving Calais at 2 a.m. for the 22-hour journey to Le Boulou near Perpignan, close to the Mediterranean coast on the Franco-Spanish border. Described as the longest 'rail motorway' in Europe, VIIA Britanica avoids a 1,200-kilometre

road journey and provides an attractive link for fruit and vegetable exporters from Catalonia and south-west France to Britain, Belgium and north-west France, as well as for industrial component manufacturers. The initial daily round-trip service operated six days a week before being closed because of migrant activity at Calais".

However, the service is expected to resume in 2017, with frequency expected to double and move to a seven day operation, allowing Sunday transits that avoid the French restriction on Sunday road freight movements. Each train is 680 metres long weighing up to 2,000 tons, with 20 of the latest generation low-floor Modalohr UIC wagons able to carry a total of 40 semi-trailers. One hundred and five new wagons are available for the VIIA Britanica service.

All types of cargo our transported by P&O Ferries as this view illustrates with a tram arriving at Hull. *(P&O Ferries)*

Potential traffic for this service is estimated at 40,000 trailers per year. SNCF Logistics hopes the trains will achieve this higher target within five years, removing 50 million lorry-kilometres from the roads and reducing $CO_2$ emissions by 50,000 tons each year."

The port of Calais, supported by the European Union, has invested €7 million in specialist intermodal rail terminal facilities as part of a strategy to develop short-sea lo-lo (lift-on lift-off) traffic. Expected to be capable of handling 100,000 trailers a year by 2018, the terminal is equipped with the Lohr system to transfer semi-trailers from road to rail and vice-versa without a crane or reach-stacker. This is the first installation of a Modalohr horizontal transfer terminal for non-cranable trailers in a seaport.

The port was redesigned to accommodate the facility, with a new zone to receive arriving trains. Controls have been intensified in and around the port, which supplement pre-boarding checks carried out by Port Boulogne Calais – the same as those undergone by road arrivals.

## LIVERPOOL–DUBLIN

Liverpool is connected to Dublin by the thrice-daily service operated by dedicated freighters the *Norbank*, the *Norbay* and *European Endeavour*. The service offers an attractive and efficient alternative route to Ireland for hauliers, particularly those on long-distance journeys that might have originated in Central or Eastern Europe, by-passing the long drive across north Wales, while conforming with the requirement for rest periods. The end-to-end journey time is thereby optimised and drivers' hour restrictions are turned to productive advantage.

Under European Union legislation, there are daily restrictions on the number of hours that can be driven, both within the Drivers' Hours and the Working Time rules. Ferry travel offers distinct advantages for freight hauliers, for drivers can comply with their required rest periods while they and their vehicle are still on the move.

The rules mandate a minimum of a nine-hour rest period for drivers, which can be interrupted twice for a total of one hour during a ferry crossing if the driver has access to a bunk or couchette.

On the long overnight crossings between Hull, Rotterdam and Zeebrugge this is not an issue, but how can the restrictions be turned to advantage on the Liverpool–Dublin service, where the crossing time is around eight hours? The answer is investment in a redesign of port facilities for freight drivers at Liverpool, where the capacity of the safe parking area at the terminal – where drivers can access showers and rest room facilities – has been doubled from 35 vehicles to 70. Crucially this enables drivers to designate the time spent waiting in the port terminal as a rest period on their tachometer, whereas previously this was not permissible until the driver was physically on the vessel.

This represents a significant improvement for the route, as following the additional hour's rest, which drivers can enjoy while they wait to board the vessel, they can continue their onward journeys into Ireland as soon as they arrive in Dublin.

Now virtually all accompanied traffic on the route can take advantage of this rest break opportunity, representing a substantial improvement in the attractiveness of the route for an extra hundred or more drivers each day.

## LOOKING FORWARD

The future for P&O Ferries' freight operations looks bright. The size of the overall freight market continues to grow and will be further fuelled by the projected increase in population of the United Kingdom – a further 10 million residents by 2030. In parallel with this, an increasingly high proportion of the population – rising from 84 per cent currently to 92 per cent – are expected to live in cities, especially London, where road distribution is key. This is especially beneficial for Tilbury, but Hull, Teesport and Liverpool are all perfectly poised geographically to help drive implementation of the government's 'Northern Powerhouse' initiative; Dover–Calais can tap into long distance rail transit developments, and by serving the two key continental ports of Rotterdam and Zeebrugge P&O Ferries can benefit from the major infrastructure developments that keep these ports competitive.

This growing confidence is reflected in the addition of capacity to the Dover–Calais fleet, the building of partnerships with third parties to expand trade and the energetic embracing of customer needs. P&O Ferries' services are vital links for regional and national economies and these strategic developments lay the foundations for a sustainable and prosperous future.

Norsky *(FotoFlite)*

# Chapter six

# Carrying goods to Ireland

The Irish economy depends heavily on international trade with over 90 per cent of freight moving by sea, and 91 per cent of this traffic shipped to and from Great Britain. So the Irish Sea has long been a hotbed of competition between ferry companies, operating across a wide range of routes. From the turn of the current century operators have faced significant challenges to their passenger business with intense price-led competition from airlines; freight carryings initially proved more resilient, supporting the Irish economy as trade with Europe increased in importance. Strong economic growth in Ireland saw ferry freight services prosper in the decade to 2008, but six years of recession followed, and by 2013 freight carryings across the Irish Sea had fallen by twelve per cent from their peak. The market has recovered each year since then, with ro-ro traffic growing by 6 per cent in 2016 and port volumes recovering to the levels of the peak year of 2007. The intense rivalry and ebb and flow of trade has seen ports such as Ardrossan, Troon, Fleetwood and Stranraer lose their ferry links across the Irish Sea, and all companies have been forced to rationalise and adapt to the changing market. Despite these challenges there is still a choice of six operators offering scheduled freight ro-ro services between Ireland, Great Britain and continental Europe in 2016.

P&O Ferries has retained its brand presence longer than any other current ferry operator in the Irish Sea market, remaining highly competitive over five decades while nimbly adjusting operations to match changing market demand, and characteristically differentiating itself by offering high-quality services with unique advantages for customers. In 2017 P&O Ferries' routes from Larne to Cairnryan and Liverpool to Dublin are strongly established and resourced with market-focused tonnage to meet loyal customer demand, complemented by slick operation of the company owned ports of Larne and Cairnryan.

P&O operated its first ferry routes across the Irish Sea when it acquired the Coast Line Group in 1971 and its services from Ardrossan and Liverpool to Belfast. A new P&O ro-ro service was established between Fleetwood and Larne under the 'Pandoro' brand from 1975, building on an existing container service between the two ports. Routes between Larne and Ardrossan, Dublin and Liverpool, and Dublin and Fleetwood followed as Pandoro followed an expansion plan. Further growth of services came through P&O's acquisition of European Ferries in January 1987, which brought the Cairnryan–Larne route and the Larne Harbour Company into the P&O fold; this route dated back to 1973, when Townsend Thoresen initiated a seasonal ro-ro service that rapidly grew in popularity to become a year-round operation. In 1993 Pandoro added the route between Rosslare and Cherbourg to its portfolio.

P&O's Irish Sea operations were brought together under the common management of P&O Irish Sea Ltd in 1998, following the merger of the Cairnryan-based operation of P&O European Ferries (Felixstowe) Ltd with Pandoro. The new company's route structure then comprised services from Larne to Troon, Cairnryan and Fleetwood, Dublin to Liverpool and Rosslare to Cherbourg.

The remainder of the decade was a period of consolidation, particularly as the group faced up to the financial consequences of the loss of duty-free sales on international routes from 1999. But a purpose-built ro-pax vessel was ordered from Mitsubishi in Japan as a sign of confidence in the Dublin–Liverpool route. The start of the new century saw the fleet investment realised with the introduction of the *European Ambassador* between Dublin and Liverpool and the *European Causeway* between Larne and Cairnryan. Port facilities at Cairnryan were rebuilt and improved in parallel. The addition of the *European Highlander* to the Larne–Cairnryan fleet in 2002 balanced the service and enhanced the proposition by providing two purpose-built vessels with excellent on-board service and – crucial on such a lifeline route – a strong reliability record.

A service from Dublin to Mostyn on the North Wales coast opened in November 2001 after a £17 million investment in the construction of a new ro-ro terminal and berth and extensive dredging of the port approaches. The new service was operated by *European Ambassador*, offering a shorter crossing, yet complementing the two-ship service in operation from Liverpool. But in April 2004 low passenger numbers and dredging problems in the Dee estuary forced withdrawal of the service. The decision was precipitated by the sale of *European Ambassador* and *European Envoy* to Stena Line, along with *European Leader*, *European Pioneer* and *European Seafarer* and the Larne–Fleetwood operation. The new owner was unable to stem the losses and the Larne–Fleetwood route closed in December 2010.

The Mostyn service had also catalysed the 2002 opening of a direct seasonal link between Dublin and Cherbourg, utilising the spare weekend capacity of *European Ambassador*. An outward journey from Dublin on Saturday, returning from Cherbourg on Sunday afternoon, proved sufficiently popular with both freight hauliers and passengers to encourage year-round operation from the end of 2003, but the closure of the Mostyn link saw the end of the Cherbourg connection. And in 2005, P&O Irish Sea also withdrew from the Rosslare–Cherbourg route; this was taken over

The *European Highlander* with her sister operate up to 14 sailings a day on the North Channel operations. *(Gordon Hislip)*

*European Highlander at Cairnryan.* (P&O Ferries)

by Celtic Link Ferries, who also purchased *European Diplomat*, however, consolidation of services was accompanied by commercial success on the remaining routes, with a record 252,000 freight units carried on the Larne–Cairnryan service in 2007.

Unsurprisingly, the years after 2008 proved more difficult, as the financial crisis took hold and the Irish economy slumped into recession, leading to a period of consolidation during which the company weathered the financial storm.

In 2010, P&O Irish Sea Ltd was merged into the wider P&O Ferries group, strengthening links with the wider group operation, and the local operations and fleet were branded and marketed accordingly. The following year the freight service between Larne and Troon was withdrawn due to the constraints of Troon harbour and the requirement to find new tonnage to replace the elderly *Norcape*. This created the opportunity to build a stronger focus on the Cairnryan route; more positively, the *European Endeavour*, *Norbank* and *Norbay* began to build up traffic on the Dublin–Liverpool service.

In Northern Ireland it was increasingly recognised that significant road infrastructure improvements were required to support the development of services from Larne. With traffic levels continuing to grow and congestion anticipated to increase, the dualling of the A8 motorway between Belfast and Larne was deemed vital to the regional economy. A £133 million scheme was developed to offer a significant reduction in journey time on a route carrying in excess of 17,000 vehicles each day. Work started in 2012 on widening 14 kilometres of existing route to dual-carriageway standard, and the new road opened in December 2015, increasing the competitiveness and attractiveness of the Larne–Cairnryan route.

In parallel with these road improvements, an investment of £15 million was made in port facilities at Cairnryan, including new a ro-ro ramp which opened in 2014. This complex project included construction of a new approach area, the creation and installation of the new linkspan, and removal of the old one.

## THE MODERN ERA

The two routes operated by P&O Ferries in 2017 are very different in terms of their product offer, yet each is precisely tuned to the needs of its respective market. It's all about having the right ships on the right routes with the right schedules.

The northern corridor carries 1.3 million units every year and the journey between Northern Ireland and Scotland is all about speed and convenience.. While the quality service and strong on-board offer from P&O Ferries is often taken for granted by customers, the shortest and quickest transit is of paramount value to them. P&O Ferries' Larne–Cairnryan route combines the shortest route across the North Channel with the greatest frequency of service and the fastest crossings. It provides services for driver-accompanied freight, unaccompanied trailers and passengers using vessels purpose-built for the route. Larne is easily connected with the rest of Northern Ireland by road and rail, especially with the upgraded A8 road now fully open, while Cairnryan has established itself as the primary ferry port in south-west Scotland. Both Larne Harbour and Cairnryan port are still owned and operated by P&O Ferries, so are finely geared to serve the needs of the business.

*European Causeway* entered service on the route as a new vessel in 2000 to replace *Pride of Rathlin*. Built in Japan and specifically designed for the Larne–Cairnryan route, she has remained on the North Channel ever since, only being taken out of service for her annual refit. After investment in *European Causeway* in 2013 she now features more comfortable seating areas, refurbished restaurants and an all-new Club Lounge. With a length of 156 metres and weighing 20,800 tons, *European Causeway* carries 410 passengers, 375 cars and 107x13.5 metre freight units, and a crew of 53.

Her sister *European Highlander* joined the Cairnryan–Larne route in 2002. Also built in Japan, *European Highlander* is six metres longer than the *European Causeway* and has a top speed of 23 knots, making her one of the fastest ferries on the Irish Sea. She also benefitted from extensive investment in 2013, in line with the improvements to *European Causeway*. At 162.7 metres long and weighing 21,188 tons, *European Highlander* carries 410 passengers, 375 cars and 107x13.5 metre freight units, and a crew of 53.

With a long history dating back to the first sailings of the City of Dublin Steam Packet Company in 1820, the service from Dublin to Liverpool is attractive to customers because, in contrast to its northern sister service, it is a longer route with a less intensive operation. The primary focus is on freight, across the full multi-modal range of driver-accompanied vehicles, lo-lo containers and tanks, specialist heavy haulage, trade vehicles and unaccompanied trailers, but the route also appeals to a discerning niche of passengers. Ports bustle with reach stackers loading containers on

The *European Causeway* can carry up to 84 lorries. *(Miles Cowsill)*

quay to quay trailers and mafis.

Neal Mernock, P&O Ferries' sector director for the Irish Sea, said: "The Dublin route is a key component of long end-to-end journeys for loads that might have originated in Central or Eastern Europe. Port facilities and a crossing time of around eight hours allows freight drivers to complete their mandatory rest period, so when they arrive in Liverpool or Dublin they can hit the road with a full tachograph, significantly enhancing the 'reach' of their onward journey. This offers substantial advantages over shorter crossings, which have a correspondingly longer overland journeys and thereby consume drivers' hours whilst incurring more road mile costs for customers. In 2016 P&O Ferries enhanced the route with a major investment in redesigned facilities at Liverpool, doubling capacity of the safe parking area to 70 vehicles and drivers can now access showers and rest room facilities. Crucially, this allows drivers to designate the time spent waiting in the terminal as part of their mandatory nine-hour continuous rest period. P&O Ferries is unique in offering this combination of a long-haul transit and rest period for practically all accompanied freight vehicles travelling to Dublin.

A less intensive service schedule also permits P&O Ferries to offer sailing times geared to meet the needs of the market, with, for example, overnight crossings timed to allow arriving vehicles to be well clear of city centres, particularly Dublin, before the morning peak. A longer ship turnaround period in port supports shippers of unusual and abnormal loads, such as concrete box sections for London's Crossrail construction project and large bridge sections for road and rail, as there is plenty of time for the complex manoeuvres associated with loading and discharge. The route carries a wide range of Irish exports, notably dairy products and temperature-controlled pharmaceuticals from Ireland, where on-board supply to refrigeration units is critical.

On-board service for passengers includes a full English Breakfast, a High Tea or a four-course evening meal within the ticket price. Also included on night-time sailings on the route is a standard cabin with en suite shower room and lavatory, towels and bed linen, and cabins are also available for purchase on daytime crossings. Coupled with the legendary P&O Ferries quality of service, this attracts a loyal band of customers despite the limited passenger capacity."

The key to a successful business again lies in providing the right ships for the route. The 166.67 metre *Norbank* was built in Rotterdam in 1992, joining the Hull to Rotterdam route in 1997 and transferring to the Irish Sea in 2002. Sister ship *Norbay* was built in Rotterdam in 1994 for the Hull–Rotterdam route, also transferring to the Irish Sea in 2002. Both have capacity for 125 freight vehicles and 114 passengers, supported by a crew of 57. Built in Spain in 2000, the 179.95 metre *European Endeavour* joined the Irish Sea fleet in 2011; she has capacity for 80 freight vehicles and 300 passengers, supported by a crew of 57.

In Dublin, P&O Ferries operates from Terminal 3 at the North Wall extension, just opposite the 3Arena and close to the east link toll bridge, two miles from the city centre and easily accessible by road, rail or bus. Bootle is conveniently situated on the east bank of the River Mersey just 4.5 miles from the centre of Liverpool with easy access to the M6 and M62 corridors via the M57, and the Liverpool Freeport ferry terminal is easily reached by road, rail or bus.

P&O Ferries may one day take advantage of the plans for Liverpool2 – the new deep-water container terminal for the Port of Liverpool – as it will provide 'feeder' opportunities for a service to and from Dublin. Costing in excess of £300 million to build, Liverpool2 is the key project in a much wider scheme being developed by Peel Ports to transform logistics in the British Isles by increasing the size of container vessel handled by the Port of Liverpool, and more than doubling the port's container handling capacity.

With a route structure that clearly distinguishes itself from the competition, and resources in place to take advantage of economic recovery, P&O Ferries' customer-led strategy is proving highly successful. 2016 proved to be a strong year for both the Dublin–Liverpool and Larne–Cairnryan services, with six per cent growth in freight carryings being recorded on both routes. Further growth is expected in 2017 and the outlook remains positive. While competition right across the Irish Sea freight market remains intense, P&O Ferries can face the future on the Irish Sea freight market with confidence.

The ***Norbay*** undertakes one round trip a day on the Liverpool-Dublin service. *(George Holland)*

# Chapter seven

# Building a better fleet with the best ships

*'A maritime innovator and pioneer, a company that delivers day-in day-out regardless of the challenges and which rides out the tough times.'*

When asked to describe the importance of the P&O Ferries brand, fleet director John Garner is clear. He maintains that the ability to consistently deliver performance is crucial and remains the key part of maintaining customer loyalty and delivering future growth.

John's key responsibilities are the maintenance of a safe and efficient fleet; he is directly responsible for 20 vessels ranging from the flagship 'Super Spirit' vessels to the often unsung freight-only tonnage. This wide-ranging role covers health and safety strategy for the ships, ports and offices as well as chartering and ordering extra and new tonnage when necessary. While these are clearly significant responsibilities, John's 12 years in the role also afford him a unique and valuable perspective of the changes, challenges and future opportunities facing the company.

Meeting customers' changing demands is a constant theme, which means the facilities and offerings on-board are continuously under review. Whether this is the retail offering on the short-sea, the overnight accommodation on the North Sea routes or the requirements of hauliers on the growing freight market, then it remains a priority to listen and take the lead against strong competition. But one overriding point remains and is emphasised by John: 'Punctuality and reliability will always remain vital and this is where you earn the customer loyalty, particularly from freight customers.'

Much has changed since the introduction of the first ro-ro ferries in the 1960s. Today the food and retail areas now resemble leading restaurants on the high street and the retail spaces mirror those at leading airports. This is in part a necessary response to the loss of duty-free in the late 90s, where traditional alcohol and tobacco sales made way to a wider variety of goods including children's items, perfumes and electronics.

Another key change since the early years has been the need to

**John Garner and Helen Deeble during the building of the *Spirit of Britain*.** *(Brian D. Smith)*

design better ships, primarily to meet the need for better freight-carrying capacity. Some commentators expected to see the demise of the short-sea ferry sector with the opening of the Channel Tunnel but this never materialised and the signs look good for more and more short-sea freight growth. Nicknamed the 'Chunnel Beaters' when introduced in the late 1980s, it is worth remembering that both the *Pride of Dover* and *Pride of Calais* replaced much smaller ships. They were replaced by ships nearly twice their size; the 'Spirit' class vessels carry twice as much freight as their predecessors.

But do bigger and better ships mean there is more growth to be had in what has become a very competitive sector? Are new routes planned to satisfy the growth in freight demand? 'There is always scope for growth and it remains vital to match tonnage resources to customer demand,' says John, as he emphasises there have been route closures in recent years that involved longer times at sea and were therefore not as profitable as those with a high frequency and fast turnaround. He adds: 'Different market demand profiles and customer trends could well help determine potential new sustainable routes.'

The basic concept of the ro-ro vessel retains their ability to deliver a fast turnaround in port alongside high-frequency sailings. John explains that the future design of new tonnage must take into consideration the need to better accommodate increased freight volumes as well as maintaining the passenger and tourist offering. This growth in freight also raises challenges ashore as port and quay facilities will need investment and modernisation. John emphasises that as freight traffic grows then ship owners build larger vessels, but critically the ports need to grow as well.

Importantly, this is not a headlong dash to a growing overdependence on freight, irrespective of good growth on freight-only routes such as at Tilbury and Teesport:

While our freight-only routes continue to grow they require significant investment. They require sustained growth, specialist vessels and replacement of revenue streams that are lost through the lack of tourist vehicles and passenger orientated services.

A key sector where Britain still lags behind the rest of Europe is support for more port-connected rail freight, particularly for the intermodal sector. While Britain's ports tend to be well-connected to the road network, most are poorly served by direct rail connections for freight. When one compares this to Rotterdam (Europoort) or Zeebrugge then Britain needs to make up ground and fast. John agrees that there is an overriding need for the government to make the case for more investment in rail freight hubs at ports to take advantage of this growing European wide trend. Hull is cited as a key port city in the government's so-called 'Northern Powerhouse' ambitions, where a new intermodal rail hub could serve the maritime freight sector and P&O Ferries very well.

The city remains an important hub for the company as it looks to extend the lives of its two North Sea stalwarts, the *Pride of Bruges* and *Pride of York*. For it was here in 1965 that P&O had its first foray into ferries under the old 'North Sea Ferries' banner. Both ships will have support measures in deck, hull and technical infrastructure as well as improvements in the passenger food and retail areas.

John eagerly lists areas where maritime innovation is bursting through. He is encouraged by advances in ship propulsion that can lead to fuel efficiencies and improved performance alongside new technology to reduce the environmental impact of shipping. This has recently been the target of new EU Directives. New fuels such as liquefied natural gas and methanol, alongside scrubbers to slash emissions, are all part of the maritime sector's own determination to clean up and reduce costs through research and development. John also highlights the growth of battery and hybrid technology and where there could be a maritime role in the longer term.

Because shipping is an international sector not bound by borders or sovereign lines then the big political question of Brexit cannot be avoided. What will Brexit mean for P&O Ferries, which connects the UK with four EU countries? 'Firstly, we will continue to trade with Europe and the signs are that this trade will grow. Shipping is a global sector that is regulated through the International Maritime Organisation (IMO), which influences and moulds EU policy. It therefore seems most likely likely that Britain will maintain policies in tandem with IMO member states who will remain members of the EU,' affirms John.

He makes clear that on issues such as maritime safety and environmental issues, the British Government and P&O Ferries have consistently been in the lead in the EU with a strong British voice through the key representative bodies such as the International Chamber of Shipping and Interferry. This is unlikely to change despite Brexit.

The historic legacy of P&O Ferries is unparalleled. It combines traditional and globally respected maritime leadership alongside a reputation for quality and reliability, which remains as true today as it was at the start. With consistent growth and new ambitions the future looks encouraging for this unique, British brand.

*Tony Lodge was talking to John Garner, the Fleet Director of P&O Ferries*

# Chapter eight

# P&O Travel

Presently, P&O Ferries carries approximately ten million passengers per annum, eight million of whom cross the Dover Strait to Calais, with the remainder being split almost evenly between the company's Cairnryan–Larne route across the Irish Sea and its North Sea services from Hull to Rotterdam and Zeebrugge. For the majority, making the fairly short 'hop' to France, lasting just an hour-and-a-half in each direction, the priorities are usually to have a meal of some sort, to freshen up and stretch their legs on deck and, perhaps, to stock up with extra supplies and gifts in the on-board shop. As all of these activities need to happen quickly and efficiently, it is unsurprising that the planning of the modern ferries working the Dover–Calais route is rather akin to that of contemporary airport terminals and motorway service stations. Everything the passenger needs requires to be easily located, while fresh supplies need to be delivered reliably so that food, beverage and retail services can all happen as advertised. P&O Ferries, however, is acutely aware that the expectations of its passengers – who include commercial vehicle drivers, a very discerning and lucrative clientele to keep loyal – rise continually. Consequently, in recent years, the challenge has been to design ferries offering shipboard experiences that will delight users and be fondly remembered, thereby encouraging repeat custom.

For ship enthusiasts, the name 'P&O' conjures up memories of the age of empire, when the company's 'deep sea' liners linked London and Southampton with the Indian sub-continent, the Far East and Australia. Yet, P&O has actually been involved in short-sea shipping since as long ago as 1920, when the company's chairman, Lord Inchcape, took over the General Steam Navigation Company. It operated cargo steamer services, mainly from London to continental Europe, and also River Thames and Channel excursion steamers, carrying Londoners on day trips to Margate, Southend or towards the French coast. Although the types of ships and shore infrastructures used to provide short-sea services have changed greatly since the inter-war era, the underlying formula of offering

**Southern Ferries' *Eagle* at Southampton.** *(Bruce Peter collection)*

**The *Ulster Queen* at Liverpool.** *(Bruce Peter collection)*

The *Dragon* at Southampton. *(FotoFlite)*

**Normandy Ferries**

big, new Channel car ferries

Expressway to Europe
Southampton–Le Havre

**EAGLE**

MARCH 31ST 1972 TO MARCH 31ST 1973
**SOUTHERN FERRIES**
SOUTHAMPTON · LISBON · TANGIER
The General Steam Navigation Company. A member of the P&O Group

freight transport and pleasure trips has actually remained fairly constant.

P&O first became an operator of roll-on roll-off ferries in the mid-1960s when it formed a partnership to create North Sea Ferries – a new and very forward-thinking initiative to introduce a year-round, daily passenger and freight ferry service, linking Hull and Rotterdam. Hitherto, passenger and cargo services from northern England to the Low Countries had been provided by a wide diversity of small general cargo and passenger ships, owned by an almost equal variety of ship owners. North Sea Ferries' shareholders were the P&O-owned General Steam Navigation Company and The Tyne-Tees Steam Shipping Company (which between them had 45 per cent of the capital). The new ferries, the

eight 'special' cabins with private facilities amidships – but the majority of cabins were below the vehicle decks, forward and aft of the engine room (their lavatory and washrooms, incidentally, were on the deck below that, between the trim tanks). Altogether, the *Norwind* and the *Norwave* were extremely compact ferries and, seemingly, no corner was wasted in what was a very logical configuration. *The Manchester Guardian* described them as:

*Simple, slab-sided vessels with only a few frills, but making both the family saloon and the lorry-borne container welcome at a properly organised terminal, they provide a full range of accommodation from cabin with bathroom to aircraft-style sleeperettes, a self-service restaurant and several bars – a long way from the grim masochistic tradition only now beginning to break*

Normandy Ferries' *Lion* at Dover. *(FotoFlite)*

Passengers enjoy drinks on ASN's *Europic Ferry* in the sixties. *(Ferry Publications Library)*

3,692-ton *Norwind* and *Norwave* were the world's first overnight vessels with two double-height vehicle decks, stacked vertically one atop the other – this at a time when some recent vessels serving British ports had little or no freight capacity whatsoever.

On-board, there were cabins and reclining chairs for 249 passengers, spread over two decks above and one deck below the vehicle spaces. The main saloon deck had a forward-facing reclining seat lounge, a large cafeteria amidships (it being part of the North Sea Ferries package that breakfast and dinner were included in the fare) and a galley, located towards the stern. On the deck above, there was a circular night-club and cocktail bar aft and

*down on the crowded short-sea Channel routes and the Irish Sea.*

From the outset, North Sea Ferries was a big success and this convinced P&O's directorate to make further investments in the ferry sector. The company's next ferry project was a route over the western English Channel from Southampton to Le Havre. As with North Sea Ferries, this would be operated jointly with a continental partner, S.A.G.A. (Société Anonyme de Gerame et d'Armencent), which had long-standing Channel shipping interests. Their planned service, to be known as Normandy Ferries, would require two vessels, the 6,100 gross tonnage *Dragon* (owned by P&O) and *Leopard* (belonging to S.A.G.A. and thus flying the French flag). The route would be competing with existing services run by British Rail and its French partners and with an ambitious upstart Norwegian company, Thoresen Car Ferries, which had commenced operations in 1964 with no fewer than three purpose-built vessels of the most up-to-date Scandinavian design. In such a context, Normandy Ferries decided to aim slightly upmarket of Thoresen, perhaps drawing to an extent on P&O's traditions of operating 'deep sea' liners. For a start, the *Dragon* and *Leopard* were somewhat larger than their competitors' ferries and with a higher level of shipboard ambience. For example, their foyer spaces were partly double-height with semi-open spiral staircases and bulkheads decorated with murals which, on the *Dragon*, depicted sections of the Bayeux tapestry. Otherwise, there were observation lounges,

woodwork and 1930s-style rattan chairs, the ferries were finished with Marinite laminate wall linings, ribbed suspended ceilings, rubber-tiled floors and Formica table tops – all signifiers of modernity to progressive 1960s eyes and relatively easy to keep clean.

In 1971, P&O's ferry operations expanded greatly when it took over the Coast Lines Group – a sprawling operator of short-sea cargo routes with some passenger services across the Irish Sea. Apart from the vessels running for Coast Lines itself, the group also included the Belfast Steamship Company, which connected Liverpool with Belfast overnight, using a four-year-old (but rather conservatively designed) pair of 4,478 gross tonnage stern-loading ferries, named the *Ulster Queen* and *Ulster Prince*. Another

The *Free Enterprise II* entered service in 1965 between Dover and Calais. *(FotoFlite)*

Four 'Super Viking' vessels ordered by Townsend Thoresen in early seventies. *(Ferry Publications Library)*

restaurants and cafeterias, as well as a significant proportion of cabins (whereas Thoresen passengers slept mostly on reclining chairs). Thus, from the outset, Normandy Ferries gained a very loyal following and came to be regarded as the most 'civilised' means of making a Channel crossing.

In the mid-1960s, car ownership remained the preserve of the upper- and middle classes and this situation was reflected in the types of facilities and general ambience found on the era's ferries – which were very much aimed at those driving their Austin 1100s and Ford Anglias for continental holidays. While the remaining railway-owned steamers were distinguished by their creaking

subsidiary was Burns & Laird Line, which ran a daytime route between Ardrossan and Belfast using the 3,333 gross tonnage *Lion*, which was of the same vintage, though conceptually more up-to-date, being equipped for drive-through operation. All three of these vessels offered rather Spartan amenities, a situation typical of Irish Sea vessels of their era in general. On the *Ulster Queen* and *Ulster Prince*, the deck heads were mostly bare steel and the furnishings were designed to withstand robust treatment in treacherous weather. As was the established tradition on the Liverpool–Belfast route, there were special cabins for police who travelled with the vessels to maintain order on-board during the marching season.

Comparatively small by today's standards the *Norwave* was to make a major impact on ferry operations in the sixties on the North Sea. *(FotoFlite)*

Inevitably, there were also cells in which miscreants were locked up to 'cool off'.

The 'Troubles' in Northern Ireland had only negative consequences for P&O's Irish Sea routes and so it was not long before the *Lion* was redeployed on a new Normandy Ferries' route from Dover to Boulogne. As the first ever P&O-owned ferry to operate from Dover, she began a tradition that has continued to the present day with only a short break in the mid-1980s when, for strategic reasons, Normandy Ferries was sold to Townsend Thoresen. The *Lion*'s service from Dover also gained a following, it being viewed as a competitive and attractive alternative to the large incumbent operators, Sealink and Townsend Thoresen. P&O's brochures for the route appear to have been aimed at two distinct markets. On the one hand, there was a clientele of motorists,

similar to those travelling from Southampton on the *Dragon* and *Leopard*, for whom catering and relaxation were priorities. On the other, P&O sought to attract a new demographic of day-trippers for tax-free shopping and drinking at duty-free prices and so various inexpensive 'packages' were introduced. These were promoted as 'Cheapies' (i.e. non-landing trips) and 'Channel Streakers' (with time ashore). In typical 1970s style, scantily-clad 'glamour' models were employed to promote the latter. Such approaches were, however, indicative of Britain's shifting demographics due to higher wages and de-industrialisation, both of which were leading to the emergence of an entrepreneurial post-working class. In the ensuing years, they too were to become increasingly important as a clientele on Channel ferries.

Briefly, in the early 1970s, P&O also had a subsidiary called

P&O Ferries *St Clair* pictured whilst serving on the the Northern Isles operations.*( Bruce Peter collection)*

The Dutch registered *Norstar* in P&O livery following the demise of 'North Sea Ferries' brand. *(Ferry Publications collection)*

Southern Ferries which ran a route from Southampton to Lisbon, Tangier and Algeciras using a purpose-built 11,609 gross tonnage overnight ferry named the *Eagle*, which had splendid facilities for a vessel of its era, including a library and an outdoor swimming pool. As the duration was lengthy, the fuel burn was substantial and so, even before the 1973 oil crisis, ticket prices were relatively high. Moreover, the Bay of Biscay is stormy, meaning that on occasion the *Eagle* suffered broken windows and structural damage – a frightening experience for passengers going on holiday. Soon, most decamped to the charter airlines and the *Eagle* was taken out of service in 1975. Beforehand, a second Southern Ferries' route from Southampton to San Sebastian was briefly tried in 1973–75, using a former West German overnight ferry, the 4,407 gross tonnage *Panther* – but this was not a success either.

In 1974, P&O took over the Aberdeen and North of Scotland Shipping Company, running routes from Leith and Aberdeen to the Orkney and Shetland Isles. Through this acquisition, P&O's ferry network was spread all around Britain with routes in every direction – northward, eastward over the North Sea and Channel, southward to Spain and Portugal and westward across the Irish Sea. Soon, the *Panther* was moved up to Aberdeen, where she served for many years as the *St Clair*.

The 1973 Oil Crisis – when the price of Gulf crude was quadrupled overnight – was disastrous for the shipping industry and for the world economy as a whole. Before this event, which forced

all shipping companies to re-draw their operational models and practices, North Sea Ferries had ordered a new pair of so-called 'jumbo' ferries for the Hull–Rotterdam route, the *Norland* and *Norstar*, offering more capacity and greater economy of scale than the *Norwave* and *Norwind*. On board, the new vessels were very similar in style to the existing pair, however, with a large Formica-clad self-service restaurant which, according to old brochures, served up the typical buffet food of the era – for instance, platters of luncheon meat, garnished with pineapple and with Liebfraumilch or Hock as the most prominent bottles on the wine list. No doubt, the ferries' passengers enjoyed tucking into their plate-loads while ensconced in an atmosphere of ambient cigarette smoke.

In the early 1980s, P&O closed down the Liverpool–Belfast route, which had experienced declining trade due to sectarian violence in Northern Ireland, and so the *Ulster Queen* and *Ulster Prince* were offered for sale. The Dover–Boulogne service, meanwhile, went from strength to strength and so two additional ferries were bought from Denmark. These were the *nf Tiger* and *nf Panther*, which were of recent construction and very well-appointed on-board with up-to-date Scandinavian design (their 'nf' name prefixes stood for 'Normandy Ferries'). Suddenly and quite unexpectedly, in 1985, P&O sold Normandy Ferries to Townsend Thoresen – which hitherto had been regarded as an arch rival. Soon, however, P&O bought its parent company, European Ferries

*Free Enterprise IV* (FotoFlite)

The *Leopard* and her sister the *Dragon* operated the Southampton–Le Havre service for P&O. *(FotoFlite)*

Ltd. In doing so, P&O became Britain's biggest operator of ferries by some considerable margin.

Townsend Thoresen had a very different way of working from P&O. The Townsend component of the business had originated in the 1930s when Captain Stuart Townsend, who had a passion for cars, decided to begin a Dover Strait ferry service aimed at motorists, such as himself. By the 1960s, the company was commissioning new builds for the Dover–Calais route, all of which had 'Free Enterprise' names with a suffix number. This indicated the company's aggressively liberal and profit-centred ethos, in contrast to P&O's traditionally rather more genteel approach. In 1968, Townsend took over Thoresen Car Ferries and subsequently also purchased North Sea and Irish Sea freight routes from the Atlantic Steam Navigation Company. By the mid-1980s, Townsend Thoresen had a very efficient and up-to-date fleet of highly

*Pride of Kent* (FotoFlite)

distinctive design. The company's interest in securing the maximum profitability led to many technological developments in ferry design and its three-strong 'Spirit' class of 1979–80 were considered the best – and certainly the fastest and most capacious – ferries on the Dover Strait. So far as the passenger experience was concerned, Townsend Thoresen believed in piling the customers in and, so long as its vessels were clean and sailed precisely according to schedule, its management was apparently unconcerned by appearance or ambience. The 'Spirit' class, for instance, had hardly any outdoor sun deck space and most of the interior was occupied by regimented rows of vinyl-covered chairs, bolted firmly to the floor.

When P&O took over Townsend Thoresen, the completion of a Channel Tunnel was on the horizon and, in response, the company was building two very large Dover Strait ferries, known as 'Chunnel Beaters', which were developed from the 'Spirit' class – but with superior bar, lounge, retail and restaurant facilities. In service, the *Pride of Dover* and *Pride of Calais* were an immediate and enduring success. On board, their passenger accommodation tended to bi-focate into rather genteel spaces forward on the main passenger deck and on boat deck, consisting of comfortable lounges and a restaurant for those wanting a quiet and calm crossing. Towards the stern, however, the situation was very different, there often being a rather raucous atmosphere in the bar. This was popular with a growing 'booze cruise' clientele, whose apparent aim was to smoke and drink as much as possible. The same situation was true of most British ferry routes in the latter-1980s and 1990s. Yet, today, with a universal public smoking ban in place and fewer economic advantages in buying alcoholic drinks overseas, the 'booze cruise' experience seems like a different world.

From 1987 onward, P&O rebranded its former Townsend Thoresen ferry routes as P&O European Ferries (today, P&O Ferries). At first, P&O decided to inspire public confidence in its ownership by emphasising its own heritage as a long-established operator of colonial liners. The ferries were renovated with pastel fabrics, brass handrails and framed prints of historic P&O vessels on the walls, to introduce what was hoped would be interpreted by passengers as a 'touch of class' – at least in the restaurant and lounge areas. In this period, many new vessels were introduced on North Sea and western Channel routes, bringing service standards more akin to Scandinavian 'jumbo' ferries.

The ending of duty-free sales within the European Union in

The *Pride of Portsmouth* and *Pride of Le Havre*. (FotoFlite)

1996, however, had a very profound effect on passenger ferry service provision and the concurrent rise of the so-called 'budget' airlines was equally challenging. Between 2005 and 2010, P&O Ferries closed down its western Channel services altogether and reduced its Dover Strait routes from three to just one.

In recent years, P&O Ferries has realised that to attract custom, it is necessary to offer Dover–Calais passengers a sensation of

The *Spirit of Britain* on her first arrival at Dover. (John Hendy)

space and light, in contrast to the cramped conditions found on short-haul jets or inside the Channel Tunnel 'Shuttle' trains. Of the company's current ferries, the 30,635 gross tonnage *Pride of Kent* and *Pride of Canterbury* have very large windows all around the superstructure. The route's flagships, the 47,592 gross tonnage *Spirit of Britain* and *Spirit of France*, are better still in this regard with large expanses of glazing and lofty deck heights to engender a feeling of space and comfort. All the lounge, retail and dining facilities are connected by an 'orbital motorway' round which passengers can quickly find the space they most like. Staircases are colour-coordinated with the yellow, red and blue colours of the P&O flag.

Throughout, the passenger accommodation is adorned with old travel posters from the P&O Heritage collection while a summary of the company's lengthy and distinguished history is displayed on panels in one of the hallways. This is a popular feature with passengers, many of whom spend quite a while reading and examining the illustrations. The restaurant service is more akin to the type of brasserie made popular by TV 'celebrity' chefs such as Antonio Carluccio or Jamie Oliver. Club lounges with free drinks, snacks and newspapers and a family lounge with children's entertainers are just some of the other activities available on-board. Facilities such as these demonstrate how ferry travel has advanced during the past quarter-century – and also how ferries and their interiors remain sensitive barometers of changing popular taste among travellers.

With regard to P&O Ferries' present approach to passenger amenities and the shipboard experience, **Dan Bridgett, P&O Ferries head of communications, said:**

Of all the many benefits of travelling on a P&O ferry, surely the greatest and most enduring is the quality of the travel experience which our passengers can enjoy. Given the physical and logistical constraints of most modes of transport in the 21st century, getting from A to B is not often much fun if one chooses to fly. On a ferry, however, the opposite is true. Many of the things which people will travel miles to experience in their daily lives – a good meal, a beautiful view, the sea air, a first class shopping experience – are an integral part of the experience on a P&O ferry. Our aim is that people should travel to enjoy the journey itself and not merely to access some far-flung location.

**Pride of Kent** (Maritime Photographic)

# P&O Ferries - The Fleet

## Spirit of Britain Dover-Calais

| | |
|---|---|
| Gross tons | 47,592 |
| Net | 14,227 |
| Deadweight | 9,188 |
| Length (o.a.) | 213.00m |
| Breadth (Extr.) | 31.4m |
| Draught (max) | 6.55m |
| Passenger capacity | 2,000 |
| Vehicles (max) | 195 cars and 180 x 15m freight units |
| Builders | Aker Finnyards, Finland |
| Built | 2010 |
| Engines | 4 MAN B&W Diesels |
| Speed (knots) | 22.0 |
| IMO Number | 9524231 |

## Spirit of France Dover-Calais

| | |
|---|---|
| Gross tons | 47,592 |
| Net | 14,277 |
| Deadweight | 9,188 |
| Length (o.a.) | 213.00m |
| Breadth (Extr.) | 31.4m |
| Draught (max) | 6.55m |
| Passenger capacity | 2,000 |
| Vehicles (max) | 195 cars and 180 x 15m freight units |
| Builders | Aker Finnyards, Finland |
| Built | 2011 |
| Engines | 4 MAN B&W Diesels |
| Speed (knots) | 22.0 |
| IMO Number | 9533816 |

## Pride of Kent Dover-Calais

| | |
|---|---|
| Gross tons | 30,635 |
| Net | 9,190 |
| Deadweight | 5,100 |
| Length (o.a.) | 179.7m |
| Breadth (Extr.) | 28.3m |
| Draught (max) | 6.42m |
| Passenger capacity | 2,000 |
| Vehicles (max) | 537/119 x 15m freight units |
| Builders | Schichau Seebeckwerft AG, Germany |
| Built | 1992 |
| Engines | 4 Sulzer Diesels |
| Speed (knots) | 21.0 |
| IMO Number | 9015266 |

## Pride of Canterbury Dover-Calais

| | |
|---|---|
| Gross tons | 30,635 |
| Net | 9,190 |
| Deadweight | 5,100 |
| Length (o.a.) | 179.7m |
| Breadth (Extr.) | 28.3m |
| Draught (max) | 6.42m |
| Passenger capacity | 2,000 |
| Vehicles (max) | 537/119 x 15m freight units |
| Builders | Schichau Seebeckwerft AG, Germany |
| Built | 1991 |
| Engines | 4 Sulzer Diesels |
| Speed (knots) | 21.0 |
| IMO Number | 9007295 |

## Pride of Burgundy Dover-Calais

| | |
|---|---|
| Gross tons | 28,138 |
| Net | 8,649 |
| Deadweight | 5,812 |
| Length (o.a.) | 179.70m |
| Breadth (Extr.) | 28.30m |
| Draught (max) | 6.27m |
| Passenger capacity | 1,400 |
| Vehicles (max) | 465 cars/119 x 15m freight units |
| Builders | Schichau Seebeckwerft AG, Germany |
| Built | 1992 |
| Engines | 4 Sulzer Diesels |
| Speed (knots) | 21.0 |
| IMO Number | 9015254 |

### European Seaway Dover-Calais

| | |
|---|---|
| Gross tons | 22,986 |
| Net | 6,895 |
| Deadweight | 7,432 |
| Length (o.a.) | 179.70m |
| Breadth (Extr.) | 28.30m |
| Draught (max) | 6.27m |
| Passenger capacity | 200 |
| Vehicles (max) | 119 x 15m freight units |
| Builders | Schichau Seebeckwerft AG, Germany |
| Built | 1991 |
| Engines | 4 Sulzer Diesels |
| Speed (knots) | 21.0 |
| IMO Number | 9007283 |

### Pride of Hull Hull-Europort

| | |
|---|---|
| Gross tons | 59,925 |
| Net | 26,868 |
| Deadweight | 8,850 |
| Length (o.a.) | 215.00m |
| Breadth (Extr.) | 31.9m |
| Draught (max) | 4.2m |
| Passenger capacity | 1,360 |
| Vehicles (max) | 205 cars + 263 x 15m freight units |
| Builders | Fincantieri, Italy |
| Built | 2001 |
| Engines | 4 Wartsila Diesels |
| Speed (knots) | 22.0 |
| IMO Number | 9208629 |

### Pride of Rotterdam Hull-Europort

| | |
|---|---|
| Gross tons | 59,925 |
| Net | 26,868 |
| Deadweight | 8,850 |
| Length (o.a.) | 215.00m |
| Breadth (Extr.) | 31.9m |
| Draught (max) | 6.2m |
| Passenger capacity | 1,360 |
| Vehicles (max) | 205 cars + 263 x 15m freight units |
| Builders | Fincantieri, Italy |
| Built | 2000 |
| Engines | 4 Wartsila Diesels |
| Speed (knots) | 22.0 |
| IMO Number | 9208617 |

## Pride of York  Hull-Zeebrugge

| | |
|---|---|
| Gross tons | 31,785 |
| Net | 18,197 |
| Deadweight | 5,640 |
| Length (o.a.) | 179.20m |
| Breadth (Extr.) | 25.35m |
| Draught (max) | 6.10m |
| Passenger capacity | 1,002 |
| Vehicles (max) | 310 cars/185 x 15m freight units |
| Builders | Govan Shipbuiders, UK |
| Built | 1987 |
| Engines | 4 Sulzer Diesels |
| Speed (knots) | 18.0 |
| IMO Number | 8501957 |

## Pride of Bruges  Hull-Zeebrugge

| | |
|---|---|
| Gross tons | 31,598 |
| Net | 18,174 |
| Deadweight | 5,975 |
| Length (o.a.) | 179.35m |
| Breadth (Extr.) | 25.35m |
| Draught (max) | 6.10m |
| Passenger capacity | 1,050 |
| Vehicles (max) | 310 cars/185 x 15m freight units |
| Builders | Nippon Kokan KK, Japan |
| Built | 1987 |
| Engines | 4 Sulzer Diesels |
| Speed (knots) | 18.0 |
| IMO Number | 8503797 |

## European Causeway  Larne-Cairnryan

| | |
|---|---|
| Gross tons | 20,646 |
| Net | 9,516 |
| Deadweight | 4,276 |
| Length (o.a.) | 159.50m |
| Breadth (Extr.) | 23.40m |
| Draught (max) | 5.50m |
| Passenger capacity | 410 |
| Vehicles (max) | 315 cars or 84 x 15 freight units |
| Builders | Mitsubishi Heavy Industries, Japan |
| Built | 2000 |
| Engines | 4 Wartila Diesels |
| Speed (knots) | 22.5 |
| IMO Number | 9208394 |

### European Highlander  Larne-Cairnryan

| | |
|---|---|
| Gross tons | 21,188 |
| Net | 10,094 |
| Deadweight | 4,228 |
| Length (o.a.) | 162.7m |
| Breadth (Extr.) | 23.40m |
| Draught (max) | 5.50m |
| Passenger capacity | 410 |
| Vehicles (max) | 315 cars or 84 x 15 freight units |
| Builders | Mitsubishi Heavy Industries, Japan |
| Built | 2002 |
| Engines | 4 Wartila Diesels |
| Speed (knots) | 22.5 |
| IMO Number | 9244116 |

### European Endeavour  Liverpool-Dublin

| | |
|---|---|
| Gross tons | 22,152 |
| Net | 6,645 |
| Deadweight | 7,360 |
| Length (o.a.) | 180.0m |
| Breadth (Extr.) | 25.7m |
| Draught (max) | 6.51m |
| Passenger capacity | 366 |
| Vehicles (max) | 119 x 15 freight units |
| Builders | Astilleros Espanoles SA, Spain |
| Built | 2000 |
| Engines | 4 Wartila Diesels |
| Speed (knots) | 22.5 |
| IMO Number | 9181106 |

### Norbay  Liverpool - Dublin

| | |
|---|---|
| Gross tons | 17,464 |
| Net | 5,239 |
| Deadweight | 6,790 |
| Length (o.a.) | 166.77m |
| Breadth (Extr.) | 23.90m |
| Draught (max) | 6.02m |
| Passenger capacity | 114 |
| Vehicles (max) | 125 x 15 freight units |
| Builders | Van der Giessen de Noord, Netherlands |
| Built | 1992 |
| Engines | 4 Sulzer Diesels |
| Speed (knots) | 21.5 |
| IMO Number | 9056595 |

## Norbank  Liverpool - Dublin

| | |
|---|---|
| Gross tons | 17,464 |
| Net | 5,239 |
| Deadweight | 6,790 |
| Length (o.a.) | 166.77m |
| Breadth (Extr.) | 23.40m |
| Draught (max) | 6.00m |
| Passenger capacity | 114 |
| Vehicles (max) | 125 x 15 freight units |
| Builders | Van der Giessen de Noord, Netherlands |
| Built | 1993 |
| Engines | 4 Sulzer Diesels |
| Speed (knots) | 21.5 |
| IMO Number | 9056583 |

## Norsky  Tilbury-Zeebrugge (Freight only)

| | |
|---|---|
| Gross tons | 20,296 |
| Net | 6,088 |
| Deadweight | 11,400 |
| Length (o.a.) | 180.00m |
| Breadth (Extr.) | 25.5m |
| Draught (max) | 6.5m |
| Passenger capacity | 12 |
| Vehicles (max) | 194 x 15 freight units |
| Builders | Aker Finnyards, Finland |
| Built | 1999 |
| Engines | 2 Wartsila Diesels |
| Speed (knots) | 20.0 |
| IMO Number | 9186182 |

## Norstream  Tilbury-Zeebrugge (Freight only)

| | |
|---|---|
| Gross tons | 20,296 |
| Net | 6,088 |
| Deadweight | 11,400 |
| Length (o.a.) | 180.00m |
| Breadth (Extr.) | 25.5m |
| Draught (max) | 6.5m |
| Passenger capacity | 12 |
| Vehicles (max) | 194 x 15 freight units |
| Builders | Aker Finnyards, Finland |
| Built | 1999 |
| Engines | 2 Wartsila Diesels |
| Speed (knots) | 20.0 |
| IMO Number | 9186194 |

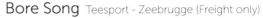

## Bore Song Teesport - Zeebrugge (Freight only)

| | |
|---|---|
| Gross tons | 25,586 |
| Net | 7,675 |
| Deadweight | 13,625 |
| Length (o.a.) | 195.4m |
| Breadth (Extr.) | 26.2 m |
| Draught (max) | 7.4 m |
| Passenger capacity | 12 |
| Vehicles (max) | 210 x 15 freight units |
| Builders | Flensburger Schiffbau-Gesellschaft, Germany |
| Built | 2011 |
| Engines | 1 Wartsila Diesel |
| Speed (knots) | 19.0     IMO Number     9443566 |

## Mistral Teesport - Zeebrugge (Freight only)

| | |
|---|---|
| Gross tons | 10,471 |
| Net | 3,142 |
| Deadweight | 7,438 |
| Length (o.a.) | 153.3m |
| Breadth (Extr.) | 20.6 m |
| Draught (max) | 7.0 m |
| Passenger capacity | 12 |
| Vehicles (max) | 303 TEU or 141 FEU/21 TEU units |
| Builders | JJ Sietas KG, Germany |
| Built | 1998 |
| Engines | 1 Wartsila Diesel |
| Speed (knots) | 22.0 |
| IMO Number | 9183788 |

## Estraden Teesport - Rotterdam (Freight only)

| | |
|---|---|
| Gross tons | 18,205 |
| Net | 5,462 |
| Deadweight | 9,700 |
| Length (o.a.) | 162.7m |
| Breadth (Extr.) | 25.7 m |
| Draught (max) | 6.60 m |
| Passenger capacity | 12 |
| Vehicles (max) | 363 TEU freight units |
| Builders | Aker Finnyards, Finland |
| Built | 1999 |
| Engines | 2 Wartsila Vasa Diesels |
| Speed (knots) | 19.0 |
| IMO Number | 9181077 |

Further reading and reference on P&O Ferries

### Books
#### P&O Ferries and other companies
P&O Ferries - Through Five Decades (*John Hendy and Miles Cowsill*) - Ferry Publications Ltd
Townsend Thoresen Years (*John Hendy and Miles Cowsill*) - Ferry Publications Ltd
Two New Ships, One New Era (*John Hendy*) - Ferry Publications Ltd
Dover-Calais (*John Hendy*) - Ferry Publications Ltd
North Sea Ferries - Across Three Decades (*Barry Mitchell*) - Ferry Publications Ltd
ASN - Road Across the Sea (*Miles Cowsill*) - Ferry Publications Ltd

### P&O
P&O Across the Oceans, Across the Years – A Pictorial Voyage", (*Ruth Artmonsky & Susie Cox*) - Antique Collectors Club, 2012
P&O, A History (*Ruth Artmonsky*)- Shire Publications, 2012
P&O 175- A World of Ships and Shipping since 1837 (*Bruce Peter and Philip Dawson*) - Ferry Publiucations Ltd
The Story of P&O – Revised Edition, (*David and Stephen Howarth & Stephen Rabson*) - Wiedenfield & Nicholson, 1994
P&O: A Fleet History – (*Stephen Rabson & Kevin O'Donoghue*) - World Ship Society, 1988

### Periodicals
Ferry & Cruise Review - Editor: John Hendy Assistant Editor: Miles Cowsill - Ferry Publications Ltd
For further information on the above visit: www.ferrypubs.co.uk

### P&O Heritage
P&O Heritage exists to preserve and celebrate the maritime history and collections of P&O, once the largest shipping company in the world.  Our unique collection of archives and artefact numbers over 35,000 items and is proudly supported by DP World who acquired P&O in 2006.  Find out more at www.poheritage.com